T0253041

Free Them All

Free Them All

*A Feminist Call to Abolish
the Prison System*

Gwenola Ricordeau

Translated by
Tom Roberge and Emma Ramadan

Prologue translated by
Anne Seiler

VERSO
London • New York

This work received the French Voices Award for excellence in publication and translation. French Voices is a program created and funded by the French Embassy in the United States and FACE Foundation.

This English-language edition published by Verso 2023
First published in French as *Pour Elles Toutes: Femmes Contre La Prison*, Lux Éditeur, Québec, Canada 2019
© Lux Editeur 2019
Preface to the English edition © Silvia Federici 2023
English language translation © Emma Ramadan and Thomas Roberge 2023
English language translation of the Prologue © Anne Seiler 2023

All rights reserved

The moral rights of the author have been asserted

1 3 5 7 9 10 8 6 4 2

Verso
UK: 6 Meard Street, London W1F 0EG
US: 388 Atlantic Avenue, Brooklyn, NY 11217
versobooks.com

Verso is the imprint of New Left Books

ISBN-13: 978-1-83976-273-4
ISBN-13: 978-1-83976-274-1 (US EBK)
ISBN-13: 978-1-83976-275-8 (UK EBK)

British Library Cataloguing in Publication Data
A catalogue record for this book is available from the British Library

Library of Congress Cataloging-in-Publication Data
Names: Ricordeau, Gwénola, author. | Roberge, Tom, translator. | Ramadan, Emma, translator. | Seiler, Anne (Translator), translator.
Title: Free them all : a feminist call to abolish the prison system / Gwenola Ricordeau ; translated by Tom Roberge and Emma Ramadan ; prologue translated by Anne Seiler.
Other titles: Pour elles toutes. English
Description: English-language edition. | London ; New York : Verso, 2023. | "First published in French as Pour elles toutes : femmes contre la prison, Lux Éditeur, Québec, Canada 2019." | Includes bibliographical references.
Identifiers: LCCN 2023009937 (print) | LCCN 2023009938 (ebook) | ISBN 9781839762734 (paperback) | ISBN 9781839762741 (US ebk) | ISBN 9781839762758 (UK ebk)
Subjects: LCSH: Alternatives to imprisonment. | Punishment--Philosophy. | Reformatories for women--Social aspects. | Feminism. | Women--Violence against.
Classification: LCC HV9276.5 .R64 2023 (print) | LCC HV9276.5 (ebook) | DDC 364.6/8--dc23/eng/20230417
LC record available at https://lccn.loc.gov/2023009937
LC ebook record available at https://lccn.loc.gov/2023009938

Typeset in Sabon by MJ & N Gavan, Truro, Cornwall
Printed and bound by CPI Group (UK) Ltd, Croydon, CR0 4YY

Contents

Foreword to the English Edition

Silvia Federici

As the abolition of the prison system appears every day more an urgent task, *Free Them All* gives us the reasons, the arguments, the information needed to not only make the abolition movement grow but to construct alternatives to the carceral concept of justice.

Focused on the conditions of women in jail and the impact of their imprisonment on their families and communities, this book powerfully reminds us that incarceration punishes those already victimized. Even more, Ricordeau shows that incarceration destroys social relations well beyond the lives of those criminalized, especially women, who are often responsible for the reproduction of their children, caring for their communities, and are the main support system for people imprisoned.

Free Them All also examines the different, alternative forms of justice (restorative, transformative) that have historically been practiced, and that movements and communities are now relearning. Powerfully written, intended to be a guide to action, this is a book we must all take with us in our struggle for a world without prisons.

Prologue

Translated by Anne Seiler

My heart breaks for all those who say nothing. Those who say nothing because it is not done, because the police did nothing the last time, because they were not to be believed when they were kids, because it's not that bad and, anyway, maybe he had the right. Those who say nothing because they know they won't be believed, because they're too strung out, too old, not pretty enough, not sexy enough, too fat, too disabled, not feminine enough. Those who say nothing because they fear they won't be believed, because they don't write well enough, because they are not white, because they don't remember clearly anymore. Those who say nothing because he's their father, he's a policeman, he's rich and he'll get a lawyer, he's a citizen and they are not. Those who say nothing because they fear that they will be blamed for going out at night, for going out in those clothes, for going out alone. That they will be blamed for getting drunk, for inviting a man home, for being on a dating site. Those who say nothing because "why say it now?"; those who say nothing because they ask "was it my fault?"; and those who say nothing because they love him. My heart breaks for all those who say nothing.

My heart beats in unison with all those who fight. Those who protest, link up, distribute flyers, cry out, come together, sign petitions. Those who fight against the rapes, domestic violence, genital mutilation, sexual harassment, the marital rapes, retaliatory rape, the murders. All those who fight and yet are disregarded because they are Black women, prostitutes, trans women, lesbians, Native women, because they are working class or because they wear the veil, because they are women. My heart beats in unison with all those who fight.

My heart belongs in prison with all these women. Those whose fate was sealed by the streets, the drugs, the prostitution, the running away. Those whose fate was sealed because they were born without the right papers, the right name, the right skin color. Those whose fate was sealed because they had no choices. Those whose fate was sealed when they picked the wrong man, when their man left. My heart is in high-security prisons and in detention centers, in solitary confinement and in holding cells. My heart is in prison with all these women.

My heart is outside the prison walls and is in the visiting rooms with all these women. Those who wait, those who are tired, those who still smile, those who always smile, those who write every day, those who have butterflies remembering the first time they visited, those who grumble but are still here, those who bring fresh laundry and send money orders, those who may never return, those who still have faith and those who can no longer bear the waiting. My heart is outside the prison walls and in the visiting rooms with all these.

My heart understands them all. Those who no longer believe in the justice of their country, those who will never go to the police because of mass deportations,[1] those who only wish that it never happens to another, those who prefer to forget, those whom the justice system has left disappointed, broken, angry or despairing, those who forgave, those who preferred to write a book, those who just wanted to understand, those who will always say "no one deserves prison." My heart understands them all.

Introduction

My Heart Has Its Reasons

The day that prisons stopped being an abstract notion to me, I was convinced that they needed to be abolished.* The idea of prison abolition did not come to me through theory, but through my gut; I did not really know how to go about it—nor even if others had considered it before me. I was twenty years old and I knew that I was going to dedicate some part of my life to it.

In the following years, I discovered, enthralled, the issues generally encompassed by the term "prison abolition," and met other abolitionists, mainly through my involvement with the anticarceral struggles. My interest in prison abolition, however, was not entirely separate from my feminist practice, which developed in large part from my own experiences of having relatives and loved ones in prison.† I understood very early on that I was living a woman's experience: although prisons are mainly populated by men, outside the gates is

---

* Translators' note: In English, the author's use of the term "prisons" should be understood to mean both jails—generally, short-term detention centers—as well as prisons.

† Translators' note: "Relatives and loved ones" is the best translation for what the author calls, in French, *les proches*. It is important to note that not all of those people on the inside are related through ties of kinship, nor are they necessarily loved by those who are supporting them from the outside: the idea of "women-outside supported-loved-ones-inside" can be a romanticized idea, and misrepresents the actual relationships under discussion.

almost entirely women. And I realized very quickly that it is these women, for the most part, who perform the *outside* tasks of material and emotional solidarity that are necessary for the survival of men on the *inside*. My feminist practice was also shaped by the reflection provoked by several dramatic events in my life. This reflection grew out of a question: what forms of reparation, recognition, and protection could I expect from the justice system? I've had different responses to this question, on at least three occasions, when I was forced to turn to the justice system in two urgent cases and was able to refuse to do so in another. However, these various experiences all left me unsatisfied. Due to the structural nature of the violence I was confronted with, whether interpersonal or from the state, I knew perfectly well that nothing had ever truly been resolved—even if defending yourself against a man and defending yourself against the state have very different implications. So I was far less interested in the idea of exercising my rights in the legal realm than in contributing, in the political realm, to the collective dismantling of the conditions that had made this violence possible.

I have been convinced of the need to abolish prisons for twenty years now. I am therefore very familiar with the dismay such a stance often provokes. I also know the one question that inevitably follows: "But what about the rapists?" I like to respond, to women in particular, with another question: "What do you think of how the cases of sexual violence involving someone you know have been handled?"

I have never received a simple answer. I have listened to recollections and sometimes to secrets. I have heard bitterness, shame, anxiety, sadness. Each woman, in her way, sketched the portrait of a justice system that isn't always just, a men's justice that cannot be trusted. Because these discussions gave rise to each woman's own doubts, fears, angers, and hopes, it was difficult to bring the conversations to a close.

All Those Interrupted Conversations
Need to Continue

These conversations need to continue since women serve, more and more often, as a pretext to justify the toughening of criminal policies[1] even when there's no direct connection to feminist organizing. They need to continue in particular because the perpetrators of sex-related crimes are, along with the perpetrators of terrorist attacks, the bogeymen brandished by the defenders of these criminal policies. Therefore, the contemporary failure of political establishments to resolve the problem of sexual violence is flagrant: the sheer number of women who do not press charges indicates the weakness of some feminists' political proposition that the criminal justice system can and should respond to sexual violence. On that note, has the criminal justice system ever protected women? What kind of women still trust the criminal justice system?

Women are certainly imprisoned in smaller numbers than men. Nevertheless, the social consequences (in particular, for children) of their incarceration are more important than in the case of men. Women are also quite numerous—I said as much earlier—outside the prison gates. Proof of love, friendship, or kindness—but also indicative of the obligation of solidarity imposed on women. So, how many more women need to be behind bars and in visiting rooms for the carceral system to become an unquestionably feminist question?

Here are a few paths for reflection that suggest that in feminism, one can draw out a radical critique of the criminal justice system. Aren't there at least as many reasons to combat "patriarchal" justice as "bourgeois" justice or "racist" criminal justice? And if one considers what the impact of "justice" is on LGBTQ people, can't those radical critiques at least draw from queer thought?[2]

Because it was created by my abolitionism and by my experiences with the criminal justice system, my feminism is allergic to what is generally associated with "feminism": the call, in the name of women, for further criminalization and tougher sentencing for crimes against women. This is the same feminism that is outraged by the condemnation of Jacqueline Sauvage[3] in France, that easily denounces the fact that other Jacqueline Sauvages are in prison, but that would never consider the carceral system as a problem for women.

Can we allow this current of feminism to claim a monopoly on victimhood? Abolitionists, like feminists, cannot stay out of discussions about the needs of women for justice or about the fate of those who are confronted with the prison system. From whom and from what does the criminal justice system protect women? Who hears the voices of incarcerated women? Of those women who have relatives and loved ones in jails and prisons? All these questions suggest that there is a conversation between feminism and penal abolitionism.

Taking part in this conversation is not simple, for feminist struggles and abolitionist struggles are often presented, especially in France, as contradictory. The first are said to demand, on the whole, more state repression, especially against perpetrators of violence against women. At the same time, abolitionist struggles are generally suspected of being uninterested in victims, specifically women. To make the conversation even thornier, the term "abolitionism" sows confusion when discussing feminism, for it can also be used to describe a position on sex work— incidentally a position rather distanced from those of penal abolitionists (on the differences between the abolition of prostitution and what is called abolition feminism, see chapter 1).

A bit of good faith and a better-defined vocabulary will not suffice to make it through this discussion, though. In fact, penal abolitionism finds itself, along with several currents of feminism (as with certain antiracist or LGBTQ struggles), facing a real contradiction: the politics of recognition fought on the terrain of law and rights are naturally accompanied by activist calls to create new crimes (for example, linked to discrimination). Yet the criminalization of certain acts, and thus of certain people (see chapter 2), goes against the abolitionist project. And this is the knot at the heart of the discussion between penal abolitionism and feminism.

Therefore, in the Heart of This Book, There Is This Knot

This book aims to unravel this knot by addressing three questions. Does the criminal justice system protect women? What does the criminal justice system do to women who are confronted by it? Must feminist struggles enter the realm of law? A systematic exploration of the protection that women can (or cannot) expect from the criminal justice system and the ways women are affected by its existence, and in particular by the existence of prisons and jails (whether they are incarcerated or whether they have relatives and loved ones behind bars), suggests, on theoretical and strategic levels, two other questions. How can feminist and abolitionist analysis be understood together? What strategies can be adopted to emancipate ourselves from the criminal justice system?

This book bets that these questions are fertile ones. It aims, in fact, to overcome the opposition between "women victims" and "unpunished men," without taking, from the point of view of women, a position that could be seen as "victimizing." If this book extensively evokes violence against women, it's because the focus of the book is on gender and sexuality. I do not claim to be exhaustive; for example, the effects of prison on those who work there, such as the guards, are not explored. On the other hand, this book does not limit itself to what its lone subtitle announces, "A Feminist Call to Abolish the Prison System"; it accords a large space to analysis of class and race, and it does not examine only the prison or the jail, but the entirety of the criminal justice system.

I write from my personal experiences as well as my activist experience, but also from research that I have been conducting for nearly fifteen years, in particular on the familial solidarity of imprisoned peoples.[4] Although I am entirely responsible for the reflections and claims in this book, I also know that my thinking owes much to my participation in anti-prison and abolitionist struggles, primarily in France and, for a few years now, in the United States, where I now live. My thoughts here also owe a great deal to my numerous encounters with feminists, the relatives and friends of imprisoned peoples, and activists throughout the world, in particular the International Conference on Penal Abolition (ICOPA, see insert on p. 21) in which I was able to participate. I thus don't claim that this book will transform political theory nor, to tell the truth, that I have written things that have not already been said, thought, discussed—by others or collectively—or written, mainly in English. That's why this book includes numerous references, in particular from the United States.

Inspired by my experience in France, written in the United States, first published in Quebec, and intended to reach a readership on both sides of the Atlantic, this book inevitably skips over some specifics in regard to certain national situations. Furthermore, it cannot be read as an exhaustive assessment of struggles carried out here or there. It is, however, born from my observation that there are certain analytic failings in the French abolitionist and feminist movements. I hope, with this book, to engage readers in debates and struggles that are taking place in the United States, and to nourish these debates in feminist and abolitionist struggles around the world.

I write in light of my theoretical and activist trajectory during these past fifteen years. I have come to rethink certain of my analyses and my practices. I have, for example, progressively evolved from prison abolitionism to penal abolitionism (see chapter 1). Importantly, I don't claim to write from a position of unerring certainty, but from one still filled with my doubts, since there is no abolitionism that is not "unfinished"—according to the programmatic expression of Thomas Mathiesen,[5] a penal abolition theorist (see chapter 1).

With this book, I am returning to those interrupted conversations, picking up their threads. I wrote it for my abolitionist comrades who forget sometimes to be feminists and for my feminist comrades who sometimes manage to be won over by "penal populism" (see chapter 5). I write it for all the women confronted with the criminal justice system, whether they have been victims, criminalized,[6] or have relatives and loved ones in prison. I write for everyone who finds themselves torn between a need for justice and an awareness that prison is not the solution. I write for all of us, for nothing will resonate as powerfully with my feminism and my abolitionism as the slogan: "All of Us or None!"[7]

A Few Words on Terminology

I am not a language fetishist. Even so, there is a significant difference between describing a person as "incarcerated" versus designating them as an "inmate." Another example: it is not the same thing to write or say that a person has committed such and such a crime as it is to call them an "offender" or a "criminal," or even to identify them by the act for which they were charged or convicted ("thief," "murderer," "rapist," etc.). Equally, I refuse to identify the typical use of the term "family" to designate the relatives and friends of prisoners—I explain the reasons for this refusal in chapter 4, which go beyond the single, and nevertheless sufficient, use of this wording by the corrections administration.

The same careful attention to word choice must be used when speaking of actions. The expression "violence against women" opportunely places the emphasis on the victims, but at the same time, doesn't it obscure the perpetrators (which is to say, for the most part, men)? Many expressions are imprecise and thus unsatisfactory: for example, "domestic violence" places the emphasis on the domestic, when it is often attributable, once again, to men. I follow the recommendation of Adina Ilea[8] in using the term "sexual harm" rather than "sexual violence" (an expression that reinforces the idea that harm exists only as the result of physical violence) or "sexual offense" (since the penal categories don't cover all forms of harm, as chapter 2 explains).

Because words can harm, if they are poorly chosen, they risk obscuring what we must think of clearly, and because sometimes we must put into words what "legitimists"* may be reluctant to name (beginning with this name for themselves), penal abolitionism has its own vocabulary and turns of phrase. It is preferable, then, in order to avoid the victim/culprit binary, to think in terms of "damage," "harm," or even of a "problematic situation"—an expression whose invention goes back to Louk Hulsman (see chapter 1).

In weighing words, though, it must be admitted that, of course, using the right words does not resolve everything. Furthermore, adequate words are often missing, for language is also the expression of a history and set of power relations. Things remain to be translated and invented. And since language is first made to be understood, I use expressions for their legibility and clarity to the greatest number of readers rather than for the purity of their meaning. Thus, rather than "person who caused harm," I sometimes use "perpetrator." I also use the word "victim," despite the negative connotations that can be associated with it, because the people who have suffered harm need to be explicitly named, and I reserve the use of "survivor" —which replaces, in feminist movements, more and more frequently, the use of the word "victim"—for conversations concerning strategies established by victims.

---

* I designate, with this neologism, people who defend, no matter the degree of complexity of their ideas, the legitimacy of the existence of prison.

This book first explores critiques of the criminal justice system from the abolitionist movement, which constitutes my central analytical framework (chapter 1). It then describes how women are specifically affected by the existence of the criminal justice system, and by prison in particular, whether they are victims (chapter 2), criminalized themselves (chapter 3), or have relatives and loved ones in prison (chapter 4). It then shows that, from the point of view of these women, the analysis of certain repressive developments of feminism require the articulation, on the theoretical and political levels, of feminism and penal abolitionism together (chapter 5). Finally, it proposes concrete pathways for emancipation from the criminal justice system and what true autonomy might look like (chapter 6).

Understanding how dependence on the criminal justice system has been forged is time-consuming and meticulous work. It must be unraveled from this perspective first to then be able to integrate feminism and penal abolitionism together. This book does that. I am a feminist, and that means I am for the abolition of the criminal justice system; and I am for the abolition of the criminal justice system, and that means I am a feminist. Because I am a feminist as long as it's necessary and an abolitionist as long as there are prisons, I hope to contribute to making, in feminist struggles as in abolitionist struggles, this slogan resonate: "Women against prison!"[9]

1

Penal Abolitionism

This chapter explains what the expression "penal abolitionism" encompasses, notably starting from critiques of the criminal justice system and from one of its principal institutions: the prison. These critiques, whether created through theoretical analysis or on-the-ground activism, provide the framework for chapters 2, 3, and 4, focusing on the ways women are affected by the criminal justice system. But first: what exactly is meant by "the criminal justice system"? What do abolitionists want to abolish?

The Criminal Justice System, the Right to Punish, and the Functions of Punishment

Penal law, or criminal law, defines offenses. In Canada, they are principally defined by the Criminal Code, and in France by the Penal Code. In France they are classified, depending on the gravity bestowed upon them, into three categories: *contraventions*, *délits*, and *crimes* (infractions, misdemeanors, and felonies in the United States). Penal law organizes the prosecution of offenses (criminal proceedings in Canada, penal proceedings in France) and outlines the process of judgment —in other words, the court that will address the violation. In France, the police court prosecutes infractions and two different kinds of criminal courts prosecute misdemeanors (*Tribunal correctionnel*, or correctional tribunal) and felonies (*Cour d'assises*, or Courts of Assize). Penal law also defines, for each type of offense, specific punishments. Those include, in Canada and in France, prison sentences and fines. Since the abolition of the death penalty, in 1976 in Canada and 1981 in France, a life sentence is the most severe penal punishment that can be given in both countries. Other types of punishments also exist, such as probation, an ankle monitor (called "placement under electronic surveillance" or PSE in France), or compensatory work in Quebec or community service (TIG) in France.

Penal law lays out the fundamental relationship between the state and individuals since it provides for the punishment of certain acts, independently of a filed complaint, even if they are nonviolent offenses (like the sale of illegal drugs). Penal law is distinguished from civil law (for example, family law or inheritance law), which oversees relationships between physical people (individuals) and/or legal entitites (companies, etc.); civil law establishes responsibilities and sets compensation, without, however, providing for punishments. The "criminal justice system" thus designates an ensemble of institutions (the police, the courts, and notably, the prison) that concern sentencing and "penal punishments." The incarceration of "undocumented immigrants" (in detention centers, among other places) is not accounted for under this definition, because this form of incarceration (holding people in detention centers) is not a punishment or sentence for a specific offense. Nevertheless, the de facto punitive nature of this type of measure doesn't exempt it from the penal abolitionist critique of punishment in general.

The theories of punishment on which the right to punish rest classically attribute three functions to punishment:

1) **Deterrence.** "Punishments deter individuals from committing offenses or from committing future offenses." The use of intimidation, which a punishing sentence is said to employ, can be discussed on the ethical level. Indeed, how to justify giving an "exemplary" sentence against a person to prevent the commission of other offenses? Furthermore, in light of the number

of people who are in prison, it is quite clear that punishment poorly fulfills its deterrence function, including for people who have been criminalized and passed through the penal system already. In fact, the people who really fear prison are those who will probably never be sent there, and it is not likely that the "fear of prison" keeps them from committing offenses.

2) **Retribution.** "Offenses 'deserve' to be punished." The sentiment that certain acts must not go "unpunished" and that their perpetrators must "pay" for them is relatively widespread. It is quite close to the desire for vengeance. The retributive aspect of punishment is thus partly related to the question of who is responsible for a crime—one person? many? an entire institution?—which proves to be hazardous in the case of "white collar"[1] crimes, as John Braithwaite[2] points out, and in the case of state crimes.*

3) **Rehabilitation.** "Punishments allow convicted people to improve." This function (which is also evoked by the term "reintegration") immediately raises an objection, since it is the acts of a person, and not their personality, that the penal system sets out to judge. On the other hand, one might object, building on earlier remarks, that punishment functions rather poorly from the perspective of rehabilitation—not very surprising, since there are better forms of pedagogy than the use of punishment.

In addition to these three classic functions of punishment, another is sometimes added, in the form of the death penalty or life sentence: the "elimination" of a person to protect society. If errors of application are set aside, it is possible to conclude

---

* Translators' note: By "state crimes" the author does not refer to breaking the law of one of the US states, as in "state crime" versus "federal crime," but rather crimes perpetrated by the state itself, as in crimes of war.

that these punishments perfectly fulfill their function—even if, of course, their moral cost might be disproportionate to the service rendered. In a larger sense, prison sentences are also a function of "elimination," because they temporarily remove a person from society. There are, nevertheless, objections that this only represents a shifting of the "problem" in space (what about the protection of other prisoners and the staff?) and time (are the people who are released from prison less "dangerous" than those who are sent there?).

It is sometimes suggested that punishment functions as a compensation for harm suffered by the victim. However, suffering cannot be compensated for, unless victims' "need" for vengeance is considered restorative in and of itself. Chapter 2 discusses this question from the point of view of the needs of victims.

Abolish ... What?

Abolitionist analyses emerging in the 1970s, notably by criminologists and in particular the Dutch Louk Hulsman[3] and Norwegians Nils Christie[4] and Thomas Mathiesen, are based on the idea, shared by certain legitimists, that criminal sentences badly fulfill their supposed functions and that they even bring about opposite effects. Opposed to classical theories of (criminal) punishment, these uncompromising analyses of the criminal justice system constitute a clear critique of crime, punishment, and prison.

Abolish Crime

In his works and through his numerous activist engagements, Louk Hulsman[5] thoroughly explained that "crime has no ontological reality. Crime is not the subject, but the product of penal policies. Criminalization is one of multiple ways of constructing social reality." Indeed, if certain actions are described as "crimes," it's because they are thus defined by the Criminal Code. In this sense, crimes (and offenses in general) are "historical constructions": these categories are the subject of debates (see chapter 5), and their evolution over the course of history reflects the evolution of the social understanding of crime.

Offenses defined by the Criminal Code are thus far from covering every type of harm: they could even divert attention from the worst among them, which are generally of a structural nature (for example, the destruction of the environment, or of capitalism, racism, or the patriarchy). In other words, the current construction of "crime" as a category largely neglects the crimes (used here in the everyday meaning) of the powerful —for example, white-collar crime and state crimes.[6]

Beyond the arbitrary nature of the definition of "crime," abolitionist analyses, and notably those of Louk Hulsman, denounce the bias that links "crime" and individual responsibility. In other words, they refused a definition of crime as the result of an individual action or individual pathology, where crime can be thought of as the result of fate, or as retribution, divine or otherwise.

Abolish Punishment

Among the main criticisms of criminal punishment, the most prominent is its punitive nature. The idea that punishment is an appropriate reaction to crime has been abundantly critiqued.[7] Indeed, if the complexity of "crime" (by considering its social, historical, and political context and by not reducing it to an individual pathology) is fully understood, the idea that punishment offers a resolution is simplistic indeed.[8] Furthermore —following the example of Catherine Baker in *Why Do We Punish?*[9]—all recourse to forms of punishment, in and outside of the penal sphere (as in the education of children) should be criticized.

Recourse to confinement and punishment has a negative impact on the morality of social life overall. Penal punishments can also be criticized for their basis in a form of delegation or outsourcing of problem solving that should instead be handled collectively.

Abandoning analysis that operates in terms of "culpability," "individual responsibility," or even "punishment" allows for the use of a new lexicon. Indeed, rather than using the words "crime," "felony," or "misdemeanor," abolitionist analyses prefer the terms "damage," "conflict," "harm," or even "problematic situation,"[10] an expression popularized by Louk Hulsman.[11]

Abolish Prison

Certain critiques of punishment focus specifically on the prison sentence. There are numerous criticisms of prison, notably the inhumanity of the living conditions of many prisoners, which many legitimists agree on. From an abolitionist point of view, prison is of course criticized less from this angle (the living conditions of incarcerated people) than from the fact of confinement itself.

It must be noted that prison has not *always* existed: it has a history, but also a geography. According to Michel Foucault,[12] prison was a "formidable invention" at the turn of the eighteenth and nineteenth centuries: the idea of punishing criminals by confining them (rather than utilizing corporal punishment) began in Western Europe and subsequently spread throughout the world, especially through colonization. Today, incarceration is largely thought of as the standard sentence (other punishments are often presented as "alternatives to prison"), but it is only one of numerous ways in which human societies have dealt with crime over the course of history. Recontextualizing prison for what it is (a solution historically and geographically situated in response to certain offenses) allows for the invention of other solutions, but also allows us to rethink acts defined as offenses.

Two political goals emerge: the abolition of prison and the abolition of the criminal justice system.[13] Although these movements intersect due to the staggering machinery of the criminal justice system established by prisons, the distinction between the movements highlights the fact that penal abolitionism cannot be reduced to anti-prison struggles nor to struggles against all forms of confinement.

Undesirable Effects or Intended Effects?

A number of critiques of the criminal justice system highlight its irrationality: prison poorly fulfills the functions for which it was designed and its existence incurs undesirable effects, as evidenced by the previously used expression "school of crime" to describe it. Abolitionists deem that, all things considered, the disadvantages don't adequately compensate for the advantages that might be drawn from the existence of the criminal justice system. Nils Christie even claims that "the greatest danger of criminality in modern societies is not criminality itself, but that the struggle against it leads societies to slide down the slope of totalitarianism."[14]

However, one might question whether it is accurate to speak of "undesirable effects" of the criminal justice system. It seems, on the contrary, to function quite well from the point of view of capitalism and white supremacy,[15] since it works to control the working classes and people of color who are victims of racism.

Abolitionisms

What is commonly referred to as "penal abolitionism" in fact groups together numerous theories. More must be said about these different abolitionisms.[16] As Willem de Haan suggests, there also needs to be a distinction made, even if there is some overlap, between abolitionist theories of punishment and abolitionist movements (which are often linked to movements for the rights of incarcerated people).

A Shared Foundation

The extent of strategic, and thus theoretical, divergences within abolitionist movements will be explored in more detail later. For now, the following five statements provide an outline for the shared foundation of abolitionism.

1) **Abolitionism argues that prison cannot ever be reformed.** This position is based on the analysis, eloquently explored by Michel Foucault, that "prison 'reform' is virtually contemporaneous with prison itself: it constitutes, as it were, its program."[17] This refusal to wait or hope for prison reform goes hand in hand with a refusal to "replace" the prison, since the goal is to *resolve* a problem, not to *replace* it with something else.

2) **Abolitionism is not a form of idealism.** According to Thomas Mathiesen,[18] abolitionism can only be "unfinished," because it does not offer a "turnkey" process, but leaves room for imagination, and is therefore by definition infinite. Nevertheless, abolitionism is not a form of idealism because it considers abolition not a utopia but a realistic objective, since it would resolve the problems inherent to the criminal justice system and the problems it generates—problems recognized by legitimists, for the most part, though they have not succeeded in solving them for the two centuries that prison has existed.

3) **"Social justice over criminal justice!"** If the abolitionist movements had a rallying cry, it would surely be this. It highlights

the social dimension of the many problematic situations that criminal justice aims to resolve that would be better addressed with a social solution.

4) Abolitionism is not naive optimism. It stems from the principle that conflicts are inevitable because they are inherent to social life. But it refuses the reification of the categories of "victims" and "perpetrators," notably because of the similar sociodemographic profiles of victims and perpetrators of crimes,[19] and because of dynamics that attribute the status of victim to that of the perpetrator of an offense, notably for certain types of sexual harm.[20] Abolitionism thus critiques the criminal justice system as much for the fate it reserves for convicted people as for how it neglects victims.

5) Abolitionism refuses to delegate the resolution of problematic situations to institutions or experts. These situations cannot be reduced to questions of individual responsibility without pathologizing the individuals in question. If each harm involves collective responsibility, its management thus must be collective.

Movements

Contemporary abolitionist movements were born during the 1970s as part of struggles that, in many Western countries, began to challenge confinement and a wide range of institutions (the school, the psychiatric hospital, and the army, among others). I will not give a detailed history of these movements, which largely has yet to be written, but will instead elucidate a few of their distinctive characteristics.

In Canada, abolitionism was profoundly impacted by Ruth Morris (see insert on p. 126), who organized the first International Conference on Penal Abolition in Toronto in 1983 (see insert on p. 21). In 2014, dozens of Canadian groups that participated in the fifteenth ICOPA proved the vitality of the movement, despite its political marginality. Today it is reflected principally in campaigns against the construction of new prisons (for example, "No on Prison Expansion / #NOPE").[21] In Canada, unlike France, abolitionist ideas are visible in the academic field as well.

The history of abolitionist movements in France is marked more by its proximity to that of prisoners' movements and the struggles of victims of state crimes. Furthermore, French abolitionist movements are characterized by their focus on prison—rather than on the criminal justice system—and their close links with anarchist movements, as illustrated by the abolitionist figure Jacques Lesage de La Haye.[22] They generally accord a central place to class relations in analyses of prison and are far less interested in race, gender, and sexuality.

Even so, the history of abolitionist organizing in France[23] shows the diversity of their strategic choices and of their critiques of the criminal justice system. Among the most emblematic are: Groupe d'information sur les prisons (GIP, 1971–2), Comité d'action des prisonniers (CAP, 1972–80), Comité d'action prison-justice (CAP-J, 1980–6), Association syndicale des prisonniers de France (1985–7), Collectif pour en finir avec toutes les prisons (ASPF, 2000–3), and the collectives that have rallied around the journal *L'Envolée* and the eponymous radio broadcast on Fréquence Paris Plurielle (FPP) since the beginning of the 2000s.

The history of abolitionist movements in the United States is much more robust. Abolitionist ideas spread during the 1970s under the influence of the Society of Friends (Quakers) and their publication of *Struggle for Justice*.[24] Another work stands out from that decade: *Instead of Prisons: A Handbook for Abolitionists*.[25] This book became—and remains to this day—a reference and source of inspiration[26] for numerous abolitionists. The defining role played by the Quakers in the beginnings of abolitionism in North America is also evidenced

---

International Conference on Penal Abolition (ICOPA)

The first ICOPA was held in Toronto in 1983 thanks to the efforts of figures such as Ruth Morris and Louk Hulsman, as well as the Quaker Committee on Jails and Justice (QCJJ). Since its inception, the conference has been held once a year or every two years in a different country, and typically brings together several hundred people from all over the world.

ICOPA has a long history,[24] marked notably by a change of name during the conference in Montreal in 1987: the term "prison abolition" was replaced by "penal abolition." This shift reflects the evolution of abolitionism, which was originally concerned with prison alone.

ICOPA has been held in North America, Africa, Europe, and Latin America. Recently, ICOPA was held in Quito (Ecuador) in 2016, New Bedford (United States) in 2017, and in London (United Kingdom) in 2018.

---

by their financing of the publication *Instead of Prisons* and by the work of Ruth Morris in Canada.

Christian involvement in penal abolitionist movements is not an anomaly.[27] Abolitionism has its roots in the word of Christ ("[The spirit of the Lord] sent me to bring the good news to the poor, ... announce release to the captives and freedom to those in prison," Isaiah, 61:1; "I was in prison, and you came to me," Matthew, 25:31–46), and the charity missions that Christian churches have always (and in various ways) carried out in prisons are in response to these ideas. Still today, members of progressive churches play a role in the development of the abolitionist movement, such as Jason Lydon, a Unitarian church pastor and founder of Black and Pink (see insert on p. 75), who practices a theology of penal abolitionism.[28]

The recent history of abolitionism in the United States has been strongly impacted by the founding of Critical Resistance[29] in September 1998, after a conference organized in Oakland, California that was attended by more than 3,500 people.

Angela Davis (see insert on p. 24), who greatly contributed to the creation of the organization, gave the inaugural speech. Critical Resistance is still the foremost abolitionist movement in the United States, notable both for its theoretical contributions (see later the concept of the "prison-industrial complex") and for its strategic vision, as evidenced by the publication that takes stock of its first ten years of existence.[30]

Abolitionist movements are embedded in specific national political histories. For example, the abolitionist movements in France, Italy, and Spain have many common points and diverge rather distinctly from penal abolitionism in the United States, especially concerning the role of race in critical analyses of the criminal justice system (see below). Penal abolitionism is also fueled by the international circulation, mainly in the West, of ideas and practices, through the work of ICOPA and other organizations.

A "New Abolitionism"?

The term "abolitionism" strongly echoes, in particular in the United States, the fight for the abolition of slavery. And for good reason. Certain analyses show a historic continuity between the system of slavery and today's prisons, especially because mass incarceration[31] disproportionately affects African Americans. These analyses emphasize that the Thirteenth Amendment of the Constitution, adopted in 1865 at the end of the Civil War, outlawed slavery but authorized the forced labor of convicted individuals. In her acclaimed book *The New Jim Crow*,[32] Michelle Alexander furthered this analysis by asserting that "mass incarceration is, metaphorically, the new Jim Crow,"[33] in the sense that prison participates in racial segregation today in the United States. Analysis on the continuity between slavery and contemporary prisons owes a great deal to African-American researchers and activists, including Michelle Alexander, Angela Davis,[34] and Ruth Wilson Gilmore.[35] The use of this analysis by activists thus links US penal abolitionism to the slavery abolition movement of the nineteenth century, and situates it within the broader movement for the emancipation of African Americans. This can sometimes cause friction with other ethnic minorities (notably Indigenous and Latinx[36] populations) who are concerned that this narrative might indirectly contribute to obscuring the ways in which they are also affected by mass incarceration. There is also friction with foreign abolitionist movements (those in Europe in particular), for whom the critique of prison from the angle of race is rooted in the colonial and imperialist history of their countries.

The word "abolitionism" and its relationship to the fight for the abolition of slavery is also echoed by certain currents of feminism in their stance on prostitution. At the end of the nineteenth century, abolitionism first aimed to abolish regulations around prostitution, and thus abolish the means of controlling sex workers. This current has since seen a reversal, as evidenced by the term "neo-abolitionism," and henceforth demands the abolition of sex work itself, now described by some feminists as "modern slavery." Without delving into debates about the terms "abolitionism" and "modern slavery," which are sometimes criticized for comparing the transatlantic slave trade to the various circumstances encompassed by the word "prostitution," the (so-called) feminist abolitionism claim that there is a connection with the fight against slavery in the nineteenth century creates greater confusion around the meaning given, today, to the term "abolitionism" when it is used without further specification. All the more so because the strategies used by feminist abolitionism raise numerous objections from the point of view of penal abolitionism.[37] Thus, for clarity (even if it is not a perfect solution), I will use the expression "abolition feminism" when describing analyses and movements that call for both feminism and penal abolitionism (see chapter 5).

Strategic Differences

Penal abolitionism comprises a number of theoretical currents that advocate for different strategies. I will discuss abolitionist strategies (and their potential conflict) by looking at these divisions, rather than at the strategies of each of these currents. Their different approaches merit a moment of closer inspection, since this book also aims to provide specific abolitionist strategies (see chapters 5 and 6).

Angela Davis (born in 1944)

When she began her academic career at the end of the 1960s, Angela Davis was already deeply engaged in politics: she was a member of the Communist Party of the United States and connected to the Black Panthers, and also protested against the Vietnam War and in favor of civil rights for African Americans.

In 1970, Angela Davis was suspected of having participated in the escape attempt of three prisoners, during which a judge was killed. Arrested after a few months on the run, she was imprisoned for nearly two years before being acquitted in June 1972.

Angela Davis then resumed her academic career, first at San Francisco State University and later at the University of California, Santa Cruz. Her work on women and race makes her an important figure in Black feminism (see insert on p. 36) and African-American studies.

After leaving the Communist Party of the United States in 1991, she remained very politically engaged in the fight for social justice. She has also been heavily involved in prison abolition, the subject of her book *Are Prisons Obsolete?* Later on, at the end of the 1990s, she spoke about how being a lesbian has informed her political action.

Can the Law Abolish Prisons?

Many people arrive at a critique of the criminal justice system and/or prison through outrage over a legal decision, or by realizing that prisons do not always adhere to the law—some are even described as "lawless zones." Naturally, such people support the demand for more rights or better "access to the law." But what if reliance on the law did more *for* prison than *against* it? One of the most powerful abolitionist arguments against legal strategy was articulated at the end of the 1970s by the British scholar Mick Ryan: "By improving conditions prisons are made more acceptable, they are legitimized in the public mind."[38]

Certain currents of penal abolitionism have nevertheless hoped to dissolve penal law using the law itself, proposing strategies to avoid using penal law (diversion) or abandoning it in favor of civil law. Penal abolitionism thus has some connection to movements advocating for "alternative uses of law," developed in Italy and later in Spain and Germany, in that these movements want to apply the existing law to dominant groups or turn the law against them. Such a strategy was used, for example, by the Syndicate de la Magistrature in France and by the radical lawyers' movement in the United States and in the United Kingdom, not unlike "activist lawyers" like Robert Lemieux[39] in Quebec or Jacques Vergès in France.[40]

Can Abolitionism Avoid Reformism?

Penal abolitionism is essentially supported by revolutionary movements, specifically anarchist movements that view the abolition of prison and/or the criminal justice system as inseparable from the overthrow of the state and capitalism, especially because of how the criminal justice system plays into their interests. Although some of these movements believe that the revolutionary horizon is not incompatible with, or even requires, the development of alternative tools to solve problematic situations (see below and chapter 6), others have a more idealistic vision of the revolution. They believe that most of what we call "crimes" today will disappear, either because they will not be included in new definitions of offenses,[41] or because changes in relations of production will lead to a decrease in crimes against property, and that a more harmonious social life will contribute to reducing crimes against people. Then just one minor problem will remain: the "dangerous few."

The argument of the "dangerous few"[42] was used frequently in the beginnings of penal abolitionism to argue in favor of incarcerating only the "small number" of people who pose a real threat to society, in favor of not waiting for the revolution to act. This argument fueled support for "penal moderation,"[43] reductionism,[44] or decarceration. Willem de Haan thus proposed a long-term strategy described as "a war of attrition in three acts"[45]: an immediate freeze on the planning and construction of new prisons, then the end of prison sentences for certain categories of offenses, and finally, decarceration (the liberation of a maximum number of incarcerated people). The "dangerous few" argument was criticized for its contribution to "innocentism": the tendency to criticize the incarceration of certain people because of their innocence (or because they are poor, sick, etc.), which indirectly legitimizes the incarceration of others. Furthermore, if the real target of abolitionism is the entire criminal justice system and not simply prison, this argument is rather weak compared to penal innovations such as the ankle monitor which could, even more than abolitionist action, bring about the end of prison.

At risk of reinforcing its legitimacy, and despite their conviction that prison cannot be reformed, abolitionists have often ventured into reformist terrain—sometimes through the desire to be heard, other times through a refusal to wait for a (distant) revolutionary horizon. They have proposed "non-reformist reforms,"[46] usually supporting the efforts of prisoners' movements, and have often taken inspiration from the strategy formulated in the 1970s by Thomas Mathiesen in *The Politics of Abolition*[47] in favor of "negative reform," namely a refusal to formulate "constructive propositions" for the criminal justice system.

Where Can We Fight for Prison Abolition?

Identifying the place to fight for prison abolition raises the question of the role of prisoners in this fight, but also highlights how this fight is connected to movements for the rights of incarcerated people. The push to construct the abolitionist movement from the *inside* (within prisons and with prisoners) and the push for building a society *outside* that would have no more need for prisons, can be seen as complementary or contradictory. The two strategies are not entirely different from one another—but we can contrast the idea of the "abolition" of prisons (destroying them "stone by stone") with that of their "dismantling"—the day when they will become "obsolete," to borrow an expression from Angela Davis.[48]

Alexander Lee, in *Abolition Now!*, was in favor of the second option: "If prison abolition requires creating a world where prisons are no longer needed, then the real work of abolition must be done away from prisons—in shelters, health clinics, schools, and in battles over government budget allocations. Prisons and the human rights violations that occur within them are merely distractions from the real problems sustaining their existence."[49] By no longer focusing exclusively on prisons, abolitionism thus became more interested in forms of conflict resolution that don't resort to punishment: for example, the "peacemaking" of Hal Pepinsky and Richard Quinney,[50] and the practice of restorative and transformative justice. This path links abolitionism to questions similar to those raised by political and international conflict resolution (see chapter 6).

Academic and Theoretical Developments

In progressive milieus in France, the term "criminology" has a bad reputation, stemming from the history of scholarship that has associated criminology with law and with providing practical knowledge to the state, including police knowledge networks. Elsewhere, in Belgium or Canada for example, the term simply designates a field of research that is multidisciplinary and encompasses the various movements that study crime and punishment—in France, these subjects are essentially reserved for sociology and political science. But some abolitionist developments are linked to developments in criminology and, more specifically, to the critical and feminist perspectives within it.

Critical Criminology

Critical criminology developed at the end of the 1960s in the United States and Europe.[51] This term, which is very broad, actually designates a number of approaches, including feminist criminology, *queer* criminology (see below), Marxist trends in criminology, and even zemiology.[52] These approaches share an aspiration beyond social justice and are based on a critique of the category of "crime," which is considered in the context of different types of power relations.

The theoretical developments of critical criminology have been beneficial to penal abolitionism in numerous ways. Chapter 6 returns to this subject, but for now I will mention that it has greatly contributed to the analysis of the role of capitalism and of neoliberal politics in the development of the criminal justice system.[53] For example, the concept of the "prison-industrial complex," developed at the end of the 1990s and taken up by Angela Davis[54] and the organization Critical Resistance, evolved concurrently in the academic and activist fields. This phrase is a reference to the military-industrial complex, a term that emphasizes the powerful links between the arms industry and military and political powers. The concept of the "prison-industrial complex" signals the development of the "crime control industry"[55] in the post–Cold War context, when the military-industrial complex had to find a new market. It also highlights the expansion of the prison system,[56] in particular the development of private prisons and the privatization of sectors of the penal system (probation services, rehabilitation programs, etc.).

Feminist and Queer Criminologies

Feminist criminology developed mainly in North America during the second wave of feminism.[57] It was born out of a critique of the androcentricity of the work carried out up to that point, which is to say the (often automatic) privileging of a man's point of view. This new current of criminology tackled subjects that had been long passed over, including the delinquency of women, their victimhood,[58] and their treatment by the penal institution. It has also brought attention to masculinity as a way of thinking about criminality.[59]

Since the publication of the programmatic article by Kathleen Daly and Meda Chesney-Lind,[60] feminist criminology has gradually gained academic legitimacy in North America, as evidenced by the founding of the journal *Feminist Criminology* in 2006. Along with other journals, it exemplifies the large amount of research undertaken in this field. Feminist criminology has never been devoid of reformist ambitions,[61] and the development of prisons specifically conceived for women (see chapter 3), to which the field contributed, reveals the controversies that run through it, as with the feminist movement at large.

Following backlash,[62] Meda Chesney-Lind[63] advocated for a deeper awareness of race within feminist criminology. That call has been integrated more broadly within the third wave of feminism, which has shown a greater attention to various power relations and the connections maintained between them. Feminism, which had formerly called for a form of universality of the *experience of being a woman*, became more attentive to the diversity *of the experiences of women*, including lesbians, women of color, and fat women. Inspired by Black feminism (see insert on p. 36), a nuanced study of the criminalization of women of color thus led Hillary Potter[64] to call for the creation of a Black feminist criminology. The ways in which feminism now examines its subject (women) is also evidenced by Julia C. Oparah's[65] call for feminist criminology to reconsider its use of the category "women"—by not presuming, for example, that all women are incarcerated in prisons for women or that all incarcerated people in these prisons are women (see chapter 3).

Queer criminology is more recent, and the term was not widespread until the 2010s. Following the example of feminist criminology, which owes a lot to the work of women in the criminology field, queer criminology was developed by LGBTQ people who called the heterocentrism and ciscentrism of the discipline into question.[66] Queer criminology has paved the way for numerous developments,[67] but already it has brought about the reexamination of a subject that had greatly troubled criminology at its beginnings (at the turn of the nineteenth and twentieth centuries) through the figure of the "queer criminal": the involvement of LGBTQ people in criminal activities (see chapter 3). This field also speaks out on the victimhood of LGBTQ people, especially with regard to criminology's newfound interest in violence in the domestic lives of LGBTQ people—a phenomenon that certainly exists, although the fact that there has been disproportionately high interest in the subject suggests that researchers' interest is to prove that heterosexual conjugality has no reason to envy LGBTQ conjugality.

2

The Treatment of Women Victims
by the Criminal Justice System

This chapter explores what protection women can expect from the criminal justice system. From whom and from what does the criminal justice system protect them? Who does it punish? What are the effects of the punitive treatment certain people are subjected to? To answer these questions, the scope of harm endured by women must be considered as well as the opportunities for women to be recognized as victims and to defend themselves—subjects that naturally lead to an examination of the treatment of victims by the criminal justice system.

A War on Women

Violence against women has been at the heart of women's struggles since the second wave of feminism and the 1970s, marked notably by the publication of the book by the American feminist Susan Brownmiller, *Against Our Will.*[1] Since then, feminist movements have tirelessly denounced the extent of violence at the hands of men, as well as the ways it is concealed, as masterfully described by Patrizia Romito in *A Deafening Silence.*[2]

"Actual" Criminality—and Everything Else

The previous chapter highlighted that what is meant by "criminality" is based on the categories of "crime," "felony," and "misdemeanor" in criminal law. If, from the perspective of social justice (as opposed to that of penal justice), the harm endured by women specifically is considered, the difference between this harm and the crimes/misdemeanors/felonies is dizzying. The criminal justice system impacts numerous aspects of women's lives, such as access to health care or education. Hence the expression "war on women," which US feminists popularized beginning in 2010 and which is used to describe the attitude of conservative politics toward women (reduced access to contraception and abortion, unequal pay, decreased funding for support systems for women who have been victims of violence, etc.).

Offenses, which are the focal point of the criminal justice system, are not all reported; for example, when a complaint is not filed. There is thus a difference between the offenses committed ("actual" criminality) and the crimes punished by the criminal justice system. This difference is often designated by the expression "the dark figure of crime." To measure it, victimology uses "victimhood" surveys that examine the offenses that individuals in the general population were victims of over a given period. This type of survey is used for crimes of a sexual nature and allows for the evaluation, among other things, of the number of sexual assaults committed each year, or the proportion of women who have been the victims of rape over the course of their lives.

The Generalized Nature of Violence

The Violences et rapports de genre (VIRAGE, Violence and Gender Relations) survey conducted by the Institut national d'études démographiques (INED) in France estimates that 14.5 percent of women aged twenty to sixty-nine living in France are victims of sexual violence (rape, attempted rape, touching, forced kissing, etc.) over the course of their lives.[3] This same survey estimates the annual number of rapes and attempted rapes to be 52,500 and 37,000, respectively. Sexual assaults (touching, forced kissing, unwanted contact, etc.) are estimated at 580,000 annually. In addition, the Observatoire national de la délinquance et des réponses pénales (ONDRP) estimates, using the results of the Cadre de vie et sécurité (CVS) surveys conducted in conjunction with the Institut national de la statistique et des études économiques (INSEE), that between 2012 and 2017, 225,000 women each year were victims of physical or sexual violence by a partner they lived with, meaning about 1 percent of women who live with someone.[4]

The categories of sexual harm used in France ("rape," "sexual assault," etc.) are different from those used in Canada, which distinguishes between three tiers of "sexual assault." The statistics also show the extent of the women's victimhood: more than 550,000 women will be the victim of a sexual assault each year.[5] When it comes to violence against women, the numbers in France and Canada are no exception. At the global level, nearly a third of women who have been in a relationship have suffered physical or sexual violence at the hands of their partner, according to the World Health Organization (WHO).[6] The expression "war on women," which may seem an exaggeration at first, is in fact justified in light of the generalized and systematic nature of violence against women, a phenomenon that Susan Brownmiller[7] cuttingly described as the "front-line masculine shock troops, terrorist guerrillas in the longest sustained battle the world has ever known." The metaphor is all the more legitimate because, as US feminists point out, the number of women killed between 2011 and 2012 by their partners (11,766) is twice as large as that of soldiers killed in Afghanistan and Iraq (6,488).

Women are not spared from other forms of criminality, including white-collar crime, but the nuance of their victimhood has long been ignored. The still minimal work on this subject[8] has shown that women, as consumers (and sometimes the people in charge of buying for the household) are at greater risk of being victims of fraud (credit card fraud, etc.) than men. Furthermore, women suffer a particular kind of victimhood at the hands of the pharmaceutical industry, which is known for its long history of neglecting women's medical needs and a failure to include women in certain drug trials. Considering environmental crimes from the perspective of women, which ecofeminism invites us to do,[9] highlights the specific ways women are victims of pollution or pesticides (even legal pesticides), as evidenced by the case of women involved in the recycling industry in developing countries.

"But men are victims too!" Exactly right. The VIRAGE survey estimates that 3.9 percent of men aged twenty to sixty-nine living in France are the victims of sexual violence at some point in their lives.[10] In Canada, it is estimated that around 0.5 percent of men are the victim, each year, of sexual assault.[11] So yes, men are also victims, and they are mainly the victims of other men. Unlike the victimhood of men, that of women is, in large part and for the most serious forms of harm, attributable to men they know. For example, in the case of homicides, of which men are victims in much larger numbers than women,[12] the perpetrators are quite different depending on the gender of the victims: women are killed, for the most part, by a male partner, and in more than half of cases by a member of their family, while men are very rarely killed by a partner or a member of their family.[13] Similar findings often emerge in other countries, and the United Nations Office on Drugs and Crime (UNODC) estimates that nearly half of homicides in which women are victims are committed by their partner or a member of their family—which is the case in only 6 percent of homicides in which the victims are male.[14]

The Risks of Victimhood

"Domestic violence happens in every walk of life." "There is no standard profile for rape victims." These refrains from feminist movements, intended to refute the long and still widespread idea that male violence is confined to the working class or certain ethnic minorities, are not entirely correct. In Canada, the proportion of Indigenous women who report that they have been subjected to psychological violence or financial exploitation (25 percent) is nearly two times that of non-Indigenous women (13 percent).[15] A great deal of research on domestic violence shows that victimhood varies depending on social class. This assessment must nevertheless be considered with nuance. A hypothesis might be formed, as put forth by Martin D. Schwartz[16] for example, that the lesser victimhood of women in upper classes results from the social and economic resources at their disposal which allow them, more than working-class women, to distance themselves from violent men.

In reality, the victimhood of women varies depending on a lot of other variables beyond social class. Lesbians seem disproportionally affected by sexual harm. Among women in a heterosexual relationship, women with disabilities face twice the risk of other women of being the victims of domestic violence.[17] The rate of domestic violence in France is close to 2.6 percent for women whose husbands have no degree or only the *brevet des collèges* (granted following an exam taken in France at the end of middle school), while it is more than 4 percent for women who have at least the baccalaureate (high school diploma), but whose husband has no degree or only the *brevet des collèges*.[18]

To assert that the risk of victimhood is not the same for all women does not destabilize the category of "violence against women." Rather, it invites us to recognize that women do not constitute a homogeneous group, and to take into account the diversity of victims—as Black feminists (see insert on p. 36) did regarding the victimhood of African-American women, notably in the context of domestic violence.

Black Feminism

Black feminism or African-American feminism arose in the United States at the end of the 1960s and the dawn of the 1970s, borne out of critiques by African-American women of racism in the feminist movement and sexism in the Black liberation movement.

Black feminism critiques a large part of the feminist movement for considering the circumstances of white women to be universal. For example, in *Women, Race and Class*,[19] Angela Davis emphasizes that while white women in the United States were fighting for access to abortion, African-American women were being subjected to forced sterilizations. The de facto exclusion of women of color from demands espoused by the majority of the feminist movement had been challenged by numerous women, notably by those who identified with Third World feminism or, for those with Latin American roots, Chicana feminism. The term "Black feminism" is generally used to cover these diverse analyses and currents of feminism.

Black feminist analysis owes a great deal to the concept of "intersectionality," articulated by the African-American legal scholar Kimberlé W. Crenshaw at the end of the 1980s. It allows for the simultaneous, rather than separate, consideration of power relations (most notably race, gender, and class), and also for understanding and combating forms of oppression endured by women of color because of their gender (like all women) and their race (like all people of color). For example, the term "misogynoir," invented in 2010 by the activist and researcher Moya Bailey, designates the particular form of misogyny endured by Black women.

Angela Davis (see insert on p. 24), bell hooks, and Patricia Hill Collins are among the central theorists and political figures of Black feminism. An important collection of Black feminist texts has been published in French: Elsa Dorlin (ed.), *Black feminism. Anthologie du féminisme africain-américain*, 1975–2000, Paris, L'Harmattan, 2008.

Criminal Justice Responses

The media coverage of violence against women often leaves one with a bitter taste. It shines a light on just how much space is given to justifying violence against women; for example, the French media response to the arrest of Dominique Strauss-Kahn in New York City in 2011, after Nafissatou Diallo, a young Black woman employed by the hotel where he was staying, pressed charges for an attempted rape. Another example is the response to his trial for aggravated pimping in the "Carlton Affair." Perhaps the most memorable media coverage was that of the French journalist Jean-François Kahn, who in May 2011 compared the events described by Nafissatou Diallo to *troussage de domestique* or "chambermaid-chasing"—an expression so telling that it was used for the title of feminist Christine Delphy's book[20] about the media's coverage of the first phase of the "DSK Affair."

The media shows the reason for the feminist expression "rape culture" through its normalization of violence against women[21] and its expression of male solidarity with the perpetrators of sexual harm, but also through its defense of those men by certain women.[22] All of these tactics deny the gravity of the perpetrator's actions ("No one died," as Jack Lang said in 2011, referring to Dominique Strauss-Kahn), minimize it ("There are degrees in the scale of crimes," said Bernard-Henri Lévy in 2009, referring to Roman Polanski), or suggest that it is not a matter of public concern ("A man's private life isn't any of our business," said Frédéric Beigbeder in 2018, referring to Woody Allen). Not to mention that many media outlets lean on the theory of "sex addiction" when it comes to rich and powerful men charged with sexual harm, and still often use expressions such as "crimes of passion" and "domestic incidents" to describe homicides committed by men against their female partners and/or their children. But beyond their treatment in the media, how is male violence handled by the penal institution?

Impunity

In France, although the annual number of rapes and rape attempts is estimated at 89,500 (see survey cited on pp. 32–3), 5,588 complaints were filed in 2014, resulting in 1,318 convictions. For sexual assaults, estimated at 580,000 (see above), just over 30,000 complaints were filed in 2014 and the number of convictions was somewhere between 5,000 and 7,000. In other words, there is an approximate ratio of 1 to 100 between the number of convictions and that of actual rapes and sexual assaults. For domestic violence, the situation is not much different: nearly 20 percent of the 225,000 women victims each year (see above) file a complaint[23] and there are about 21,000 convictions for domestic violence each year.[24]

France is far from being an exception. In Canada, the rate of sexual assaults reported to the police is estimated at 5 percent.[25] In the United States, less than a quarter of physical violence within relationships is reported to the police, and charges are pressed in only 7.3 percent of cases.[26] In fact, numerous studies show that, throughout the world, crimes in which women are victims are underreported and lead to fewer prosecutions than other crimes of the same gravity. The permissiveness that surrounds violence against women is widespread and results from a long history of male domination. It also stems from the ways in which laws perpetuate that domination (see, later on, women and self-defense), but also the values and beliefs that guide courts' rulings, like the myth of the "crime of passion"—how certain kinds of male violence are "excused" in the name of "passion," when it is in fact only a matter of violence.

Research on sentencing[27] shows how sentences are influenced by victims' characteristics, including their ethnic origin, their age, their behavior (for example, drug use) or their reputation.[28] In other words, crimes committed against certain women (those who are poor, ethnic minorities, or sex workers) are punished less severely than others. In the United States, the case of Black women is particularly well documented, thanks to the foundational work of Angela Davis[29] and the more recent work of Beth Richie.[30] Another example is the murders and disappearances of Indigenous women in Canada.[31] Although the number of Indigenous women disappeared or murdered in the past thirty years is generally cited as 1,200,[32] exact statistics on the phenomenon don't exist, precisely because of the negligence of authorities when it comes to Indigenous women, even if it has been shown that they are victims in disproportionate numbers compared to other women.

To summarize, only certain harm against women interests the criminal justice system: the harm defined by the system as misdemeanors, felonies, or crimes. But only a portion of the offenses committed are brought before the system (depending on whether or not a complaint is filed)[33] and of those, not all are punished (depending on whether charges are prosecuted). The people judged by the courts, and especially those who are convicted, at the end of criminal proceedings, thus represent only a tiny portion of those who harm women. The majority of perpetrators never face consequences.

Who Gets Convicted?

Just as the feminist movement asserts that there is no standard profile for women victims, the same is generally claimed when it comes to perpetrators. This is certainly true. Nevertheless, depending on their ethnic origin, class, or profession, not all perpetrators run the same risk of being charged and convicted. Indeed, these characteristics influence the victims' decisions to file a complaint or not, but also influence the judges' decision on whether to prosecute and sentence. It is also known that those convicted of rape in France are almost exclusively working class.[34]

The profiles of convicted people also show how race shapes criminal proceedings. The overrepresentation of Black men among incarcerated people is well documented.[35] In the cases of those charged with sexual harm, the influence of the racist "Black rapist" myth must be examined. Denounced by Angela Davis in *Women, Race and Class*, this phenomenon relies on the fact that Black men were—and still are—considered a sexual threat to white women. In the United States, this myth has translated concretely into countless African-American men being unfairly convicted, and has served to justify the lynching of some of them, primarily between 1880 and 1930. This myth still holds power today, as evidenced by the overrepresentation of African-American men[36] on the registry of people convicted for sex-related offenses in the United States, which was created as part of Megan's Laws (see later and insert below).

The fact that convictions disproportionately target certain populations (and certain men) rattled the feminist movement in the wake of the first rape sentences handed down by the

---

Megan's Laws (United States)

Megan's Laws were instated in the United States in 1994. This set of laws owes its name to Megan Kanka, a young girl in New Jersey killed that year by a man already convicted twice for the sexual abuse of a minor.

These laws require that all people convicted of crimes of a sexual nature be entered in a police registry. They also require the dissemination to the public (through social networks, websites, local newspapers, etc.) of details (their name, address, dates of incarceration, the nature of the crime for which they were convicted, and their photograph) of all people on the registry.

Inclusion on the registry generally lasts at least ten years and can be indefinite. People on the registry report being regularly harassed by strangers and having difficulty finding jobs or places to live. As shown in the documentary *Pervert Park* (Frida and Lasse Barkfors, 2014), certain people on the registry find refuge in housing projects or mobile home parks, often organized with the help of churches, where all the inhabitants are registered sex offenders.

In 2016, 859,500 people were on these registries.

Courts of Assize in France (see chapter 5). Recognizing that the judiciary system is uncompromising for certain people fueled support for the Swiss academic, philosopher, and writer Tariq Ramadan after his incarceration in France in February 2018 following his indictment for three rapes. Although being taken into custody is not exceptional for such a case, Tariq Ramadan did not benefit from the preferential treatment he might have had access to if he had not been known primarily as a Muslim and Arab figure. That Tariq Ramadan constitutes the most visible "spoils of war" of the #MeToo movement in France highlights the fact that although the criminal justice system largely serves the interests of the patriarchy in leaving crimes of men largely unpunished, it also uses women as a pretext to serve the interests of the bourgeoisie and white supremacy.

Criminal Justice: A Hostile Institution for Men?

In response to feminist calls for fairness and equal treatment, certain masculinists[37] *also* demand equal treatment within the prison population. Beyond the preposterousness of such a demand,[38] masculinists have succeeded, in recent years, in spreading the theory that the legal system is "under the influence" (of feminism) and, thus, increasingly hostile to men. The inverse is clearly demonstrated through the impunity that surrounds the vast majority of crimes committed against women, and through the permissiveness that characterizes many sentences for such crimes.

In France, masculinists worry in particular about the increasing feminization of the judicial system. It is true that nearly three new judges in four are women and more than 63 percent of judges are now women. Nothing, however, supports the theory that female judges are more severe toward men than male judges. As Arthur Vuattoux[39] shows in his overview on US sentencing research, no difference in the ways that men and women are judged has been identified—much in the same way that sentences vary little depending on the ethnic origins of the judges, and that members of ethnic minorities cannot hope for any favorable treatment from non-white judges.

The Effects of Punitive Treatment

Chapter 5 explores alternatives to the punitive treatment of offenses proposed by abolitionism, but first the effects of this type of treatment on convicted people must be examined.

Proof by Recidivism

Chapter 1 explored penal abolitionism's critique of the claim that prison allows for the rehabilitation of people confined there. The statistics on recidivism reveal a glimpse of the failure of the penal system on this front. But only a glimpse, because they only take into account, by definition, the acts brought before the system. These statistics must always be taken with a grain of salt. What is collectively understood by "recidivism" is the committing of another offense, while the legal definition can be more restrictive.[40]

Although those convicted of sex-related offenses reoffend less than perpetrators of other types of offenses, they tend to reoffend for the same type of offense. As much research shows, and as legitimists agree, it is difficult to prove that time in prison diminishes the risk of recidivism. Additionally, many studies suggest the limited or null effects of the treatments offered to individuals convicted of sexual harm (for example, see a 2016 study by the Bureau of Crime Statistics and Research in New South Wales, Australia, showing a similar rate of recidivism (20.3 percent in the following year) for men given a conditional sentence and those sentenced to prison).[41]

Furthermore, many abolitionists have argued that incarceration is a form of vengeance against perpetrators of sex-related crimes because of the prevalence of sexual harm in prison, and the fact that those sentenced for these types of offense are often the victims of it. This argument is supported by the British abolitionist activist Joe Sim[42] and by Catherine Baker, who writes: "Whether the rapist is sequestered, humiliated, beaten by his fellow prisoners, or condemned to suicide will not protect anyone from rape."[43] This is true.

My own research[44] on prisons allows me to bring some nuance to this argument. First, the representation of rape in prison as a generalized phenomenon is largely influenced by the US media, including films. It is a fact that in prison, as in many other predominantly male environments, the fear of rape is widespread and numerous forms of sexual harm do exist. While it is fair to acknowledge that in prison perpetrators of sex-related crimes face an increased risk of becoming a victim of sexual harm themselves, it is at least as much of a risk for any woman (and trans women in particular) in prison, and any incarcerated man who does not adhere to the classical criteria of masculinity (for example, gay men). In sum, focusing on the sexual harm that perpetrators of sex-related crimes face in prison seems to miss the point of the central abolitionist argument: prison does not work for anyone.

Register, Monitor: To What End?

The proportion of men who report having sexual fantasies involving children is estimated to be between 0.2 percent and 2.4 percent.[45] This statistic highlights what the moral panic surrounding pedophilia starting in the 1990s often glosses over: many people who have pedophilic fantasies never act on them and are even aware of the problematic nature of these fantasies. The scarcity of resources offered to those seeking help is in large part due to the punitive approach to the subject, although some positive progress has been made on this front in certain European countries.[46]

The specter of pedophilia has served as a pretext for a number of criminal justice innovations in the West,[47] beginning with adding an increasing number of people to sex-offender registries. In France, a law passed on June 17, 1998, created the Fichier national automatisé des empreintes génétiques (FNAEG, National Digital Registry of Genetic Fingerprints), requiring the genetic fingerprinting of all people convicted of sex-related offenses. The FNAEG was quickly expanded to other types of offenses, and a law passed on November 15, 2001, that requires the registration of anyone convicted of serious offenses against the person. The Fichier judiciaire automatisé des auteurs d'infractions sexuelles ou violentes (FIJAISV, Judicial Digital Registry of Sexual or Violent Offenders), created in 2004, followed a similar progression. At first limited to perpetrators of sexual abuse of minors, it was expanded in 2005 to perpetrators of violent offenses.

The Islamist terrorist has recently overshadowed the pedophile as the most dangerous threat in the Western public mind. Both have served to legitimize the creation of new categories of offenses. Much like the criminalization of possessing child pornography, regularly consulting terrorist sites has become an offense in France, but it must be "accompanied by evidence of the adherence to an ideology expressed on the platform in question."[48] Even if there is a valid argument to be made for the protection of victims, there is no proven link between consulting an image and reproducing the acts represented in it. Such a policy does nothing to combat the social conditions that lead to pedophilia or Islamist terrorism, or even forms of voyeurism (which is morally reprehensible, but should it fall under the jurisdiction of the criminal justice system?). Worse, considering the powerful draw of illicit sexual matters, as pointed out by Amy Adler[49] or Chloë Taylor,[50] the crackdown caused by moral panic surrounding pedophilia might in fact lead to opposite results from what is intended.

Much research shows that punitive approaches to sexual harm are not effective.[51] Furthermore, such approaches are based increasingly on the notion that perpetrators will always be likely to reoffend, which is far from the case.[52] In the United States, the coercive measures used for those convicted of crimes of a sexual nature, in particular in the case of Megan's Laws, have not led to a reduction in pedophilic crimes. Additionally, research shows that the rates of recidivism are similar for those on registries and those who are not.[53]

Not only is this approach ineffective, but it is dangerous, as noted by Erica R. Meiners: Sex Offender Registries "participate in ignoring and even protecting a central site of sexualized violence, the patriarchal family."[54] Registries actually reinforce the widespread idea that women (and children) must be wary of people outside of their circle, while the perpetrators of sexual harm are in fact most often people who are close to the victims.[55] Another argument against these registries is that a certain number of the acts for which people are added to the registry are consensual sexual acts (exposing someone to HIV,[56] sexual relations with a person under 17 years old, paid sexual activity, etc.). Setting aside the controversy over using the notion of consent to legally define sexual harm, it can still be noted that not taking it into account results in the registration of a significant number of sex workers and LGBTQ people because of their sexual activities, and not because of any involvement in nonconsensual acts.[57]

The Criminalization of Self-Defense by Women

In recent years, cases of women imprisoned for killing an attacker or a violent male partner have drawn public attention and fueled feminist protests. In the United States, notable cases include CeCe McDonald (see insert on p. 48) and Marissa Alexander.[58] The neglect of the law to take into account what led these women to resort to violent self-defense provoked a profound sense of injustice among many women. This same sense of injustice is at the root of protests in France over the conviction (upheld on appeal in December 2015) of Jacqueline Sauvage to a ten-year prison sentence for the homicide of her husband after forty-seven years of marriage, during which he had been violent toward her and had raped her daughters.[59]

Many incarcerated women have been victims of domestic violence (see chapter 3), but not all are in prison for defending themselves. Assessing the number of women incarcerated for acts of self-defense is complex, and there are very few quantitative studies on this subject. The estimates conducted in the United States are difficult to transpose elsewhere and are also starting to become outdated. Nevertheless, they confirm what is already known about prisons for women: the phenomenon is not anecdotal. Feminist movements in the United States often cite a survey conducted by the Department of Corrections and Community Supervision in the state of New York, which estimated in 2005 that 67 percent of women imprisoned for the homicide of a relative had been the victim of that person. For the United States as a whole, Elizabeth Dermody Leonard estimates the number at 4,500.[60]

These numbers reveal a distinct failure of the law to take into account the nuances of how women experience violence, and to make adequate provision for them in the legally defined conditions under which self-defense is recognized as a legitimate act. In France, the definition of self-defense is very narrow. An attack must be happening at the time of the incident, must be substantial in nature, and must be unjustified (in plain language: legitimate self-defense against the police does not exist). Additionally, the defense must be necessary (there must be an absence of other means to avoid danger), proportional (no recourse to a weapon in the event of an unarmed attack, for example), and simultaneous (it is unlawful to pursue an attacker who flees, for example).

This definition of legitimate self-defense poorly corresponds to the context of domestic violence in which victims can feel constantly under threat and then perhaps kill their attacker outside of a situation of imminent danger. In the 1980s, the definition of "battered-woman syndrome" allowed, in the Anglo-Saxon world, for a better understanding of these homicides. First theorized by Leonore Walker[61] and Cynthia Gillespie,[62] this syndrome, related to the expression "mental control," is similar to a post-traumatic state in which the person feels continually threatened and suffers from associated issues, such as trouble concentrating or hyper-vigilance.

The Canadian judicial system acknowledged battered-woman syndrome rather quickly. In 1990, it pronounced the first acquittal of a woman, Angélique Lyn Lavallee, who had been charged with homicide of a violent spouse. Subsequently, it recognized the notion of "deferred self-defense" (which also exists, to a lesser extent, in Swiss law), meaning the exercise of legitimate self-defense outside of immediate danger, which takes into consideration the particular circumstances of female victims of violent men.

In the United States, women who have been incarcerated for self-defense, notably in California, can be credited for improving the legal system by forcing it to consider the situation of battered women. Organized by Brenda Clubine,[63] incarcerated women in California created Convicted Women Against Abuse (CWAA) in 1989. This group helped the "battered-woman defense" to be accepted by the state of California in 1992. It then worked to have convictions handed down prior to the recognition of battered-woman syndrome reexamined. In 2002, California became the first state to allow for the revision of convictions on that basis. In 2012, since fewer than twenty-five women had been liberated between 2002 and 2010 while the number of incarcerated women in California who had been the victims of domestic violence was estimated to be about 7,000, a new law was adopted[64] in order to allow for the early release of more women. But California is an exception in the United States, and the fight for women criminalized in a context of domestic violence continues, led in large part by organizations of women who find themselves in this situation, such as Battered Women of Texas, and coalitions such as Survived and Punished.

In France, spurred notably by protests in support of Jacqueline Sauvage, especially at the beginning of 2016, there have been calls for a modified definition of legitimate self-defense and the recognition of battered-woman syndrome, which would lead to a mitigation of criminal liability. The proposed law, put forward on March 8, 2016, by MP Valérie Boyer (Republican) was not, however, adopted. The rationale for opposing the proposition was that it is forbidden under French law to treat men and women differently, and that it is

---

CeCe McDonald (born in 1989)

In June 2011, in Minneapolis, CeCe McDonald, a young trans and African-American woman who was twenty-two years old at the time, was attacked by a man. She defended herself with a knife and the man died from his wounds. CeCe McDonald then received a twenty-year prison sentence. Protests over the transphobic and racist nature of the attack finally led to a reduced sentence of forty-one months.

CeCe McDonald spoke out against her prison conditions, in particular her placement in correctional institutions for men. The movement to support CeCe McDonald received a great deal of assistance from the trans actress and activist Laverne Cox.

CeCe McDonald was released in January 2014 after nineteen months in prison. She is still an activist and has become an important figure of trans liberation movements.

A documentary, *FREE CeCe* (2016), co-produced by Laverne Cox, tells her story, but also demonstrates the scope of violence committed against racialized trans women.

---

already possible for verdicts to take into account the particular circumstances of women who are victims of domestic violence (as exemplified by the acquittal of Alexandra Lange[65]) based on "state of necessity."[66]

Even if there were not reason to be wary of the long history of state manipulation of women's fight against male violence (see chapter 5), the simple acknowledgment of battered-woman syndrome within the interpretation of legal self-defense would still be insufficient. Indeed, as emphasized by Sharon Agella Allard,[67] its definition rests in large part on racial stereotypes associated with white women and therefore does not allow for the recognition of the ways in which women of color react to domestic violence—as in the case of African-American women affected by the "strong Black woman" syndrome.[68]

Victims of the Criminal Justice System

In 1977, the Norwegian abolitionist Nils Christie expressed, in his article "Conflicts as Property,"[69] a critique of the criminal justice system that has been evoked frequently since: the criminal justice system "steals" conflicts from individuals, conflicts that are by nature "valuable." I am not sure that conflicts can always be deemed as "valuable," because the circumstances vary—and are sometimes extreme. Nevertheless, his analysis hits the nail on the head: the criminal justice system's handling of a problematic situation means that the community loses the opportunity to change the social conditions that made the conflict possible in the first place. Furthermore, the criminal justice system does not respond, by definition, to the clearly documented needs of victims to regain control over their lives.

Criminal Proceedings and the Risk of
"Secondary Victimization"

The rise in power of victims' rights movements (see chapter 5) starting in the 1970s in the United States and Canada, and more recently in France, has led to certain improvements in the treatment of victims by the criminal justice system, principally during their police intake. One of the changes made to the criminal justice system is the introduction of restorative justice practices in France and in other Western countries (see chapter 6). Even so, these developments do not fundamentally negate the system's shortcomings from the perspective of victims' treatment.

The criminal justice system determines the classification of crimes and thus their gravity ("rape" versus "sexual assault")—which Nils Christie describes as a "theft" of harm[70] because said classification does not always correspond to the experience of the victim themselves. The "theft" is so complete that the victim must often be represented by a lawyer. By submitting their story of harm to the criminal justice system, the victim takes on the additional risk that the harm done to them will not be recognized as such and that their word will thus be called into question. The victim must prove that the harm took place, in other words detail it and provide contextual elements that are often personal, and this must generally be done in public or, at the very least, in front of a jury they have not chosen. They are also required to act like a victim, meaning they must conform to what is expected of an "ideal victim."[71]

The criminal process has come under heavy critique for its timeline: the pace of legal proceedings never perfectly coincides with the phases through which a victim passes, and this is true no matter the type of victim (whether someone has experienced the loss of a loved one or suffered sexual harm, etc.). One might want to discuss the events during certain periods and not others. One might also feel able to be in the presence of the person who has caused harm at certain moments, and not at others.

The nature of the criminal trial encourages victims to exaggerate their victimhood and their suffering, since these are expected of a "real" victim. Trials also encourage the accused who plead innocent to use every means available under the law in their defense. Along these lines, a recent event in France seems exemplary to me of a misguided feminist tendency: in January 2018, Jonathann Daval's defense following his indictment for the murder of his wife elicited outrage for citing the supposed violence she herself committed, despite an exhaustive police investigation that revealed no such violence. These reactions seem rather misplaced to me. I do not see how one can demand or even hope for people to become morally irreproachable once their crime is discovered, nor for them to be fully aware of the harm they have caused or how it fits into structural power relations. The duplicity of his behavior after the "disappearance" of his spouse[72] in October 2017, and the misogyny of his defense, for which he was criticized, are par for the course in courts. But the common means a person uses to defend themselves, in their heart, from less serious things are rarely any better, and resemble those used to minimize harm suffered by others; for example, when an insult is thought of as "deserved," or when theft is "not really theft" because there is legitimate need, or when a traffic violation is justified due to personal circumstances (delay, irritation, etc.).

The structure of the trial shapes the defense of those being prosecuted, especially the way in which they express themselves. Rarely does a trial allow for the victim to hear something that might be useful to them, since any hint of remorse is typically prompted by lawyers. Trials in the United States are even more troubling on this front: the accused rarely speak, since the Fifth Amendment of the Constitution protects against self-incrimination and thus allows them not to take the stand. Even those convicted rarely express remorse, because remorse often has little effect on the sentence due to the system's "mandatory minimum sentences"[73] and "sentencing guidelines."[74]

Taken together, these critiques highlight the risk of "secondary victimization"[75] through criminal proceedings and signal a need for more emphasis on the needs of victims. Ruth Morris, who greatly contributed to the development of transformative justice (see insert on p. 126), describes five needs: 1) answers to their questions, even the most trivial, about the facts of their situation; 2) recognition of their harm; 3) safety; 4) restitution; 5) to be able to give meaning to what they have suffered.[76] Do the trial and potential sentencing fulfill these needs?

Perhaps for certain victims: the criminal trial does allow for a form of recognition of the harm suffered, and the perpetrator's confinement can bring a sense of safety—although it can also fuel fears of future vengeance, and fear can endure in the absence of real danger. Sometimes the accused even manages, in this setting more suited to dispute than reconciliation, to speak words that bring solace to the victim. Such trials do exist. I have heard children forgive the man who killed their father after he recounted the unfortunate circumstances of his life and expressed very sincere apologies. I have heard a mother tell a young man who had driven under the influence of alcohol and killed her son that she thought each day of his parents, who, in their own way, had also lost a son. Such moments do exist in court. But they happen largely by accident and depend on the temperaments of the accused and the victims (and often of their families and friends), not to mention the judges who sometimes forget the punitive nature of their role.

But criminal proceedings can be quite removed from the needs of a victim. There is no guarantee that they will be recognized as victims (sometimes perpetrators are acquitted on a technicality), and a conviction does not guarantee progress for the victim in their own recovery. Even the sentence can be deceiving: how can it be commensurate with the victim's pain (especially in the case of a homicide)? Furthermore, victims often feel ambivalent about the sentence, especially when the perpetrator is a family member ("He's also the father of my children") or because their background elicits compassion ("He's a lost soul; he should have been helped, not sent to prison").

The Dependency on Criminal Courts

I will save for chapter 6 my response to a very practical question: as an abolitionist, should one file a complaint? From the perspective of the victims, the critique of the criminal justice system offers a few general insights.

Ruth Morris describes our society as "penaholic" (a portmanteau of penal and alcoholic) to emphasize our dependency on the criminal justice system.[77] This is dangerous, because it goes hand in hand with "judiciarism," the belief that the ability of the law to solve problems outweighs its reinforcement of power relations. Additionally, this dependency tends to solidify the opinion, unfortunately already widespread, that a trial is the only way for an individual to be recognized as a victim and to begin the work of recovery or mourning. But, in a number of cases, there is no trial, either because no charges were brought (for lack of evidence) or the perpetrator was never found or is dead, or else because they are deemed not responsible or incompetent for mental health reasons. And judges or juries may acquit, sometimes based on a technicality.

In light of the rich history of radical self-defense,[78] this dependency on the criminal justice system is unfortunate because it creates a role of "victim" for women that is not entirely removed from the patriarchal system, as described by Gail Pheterson: "The woman caught in the act of independence is ... suspect and the fact of being the victim of violence sometimes constitutes her only hope of redemption. The criminal policies themselves often stipulate that the status of victim is the sole legitimate excuse in case of an illegal action or for access to resources usually reserved for the privileged."[79]

3

Criminalized Women

The previous chapter showed that women are poorly protected by the criminal justice system. Does this mean that the system is completely uninterested in them? Considering their small proportion among criminalized people, it is worth asking: do women avoid criminal sentencing? The response to this question naturally leads to another: what are the characteristics of criminalized women? The answer reveals the reason for the lack of political solidarity with these women within feminist movements—reasons that chapter 5 goes into in more detail. When criminalized women are considered within an abolitionist framework, other questions arise: How do the sentences served affect these women? What solidarities can they count on? Should women in prison be treated differently than men? These are some of the questions this chapter will try to answer.

Criminalized Women: Anomalies?

Women make up a small minority of criminalized people. In Canada, they are 6 percent of the federal prison population.[1] In France, on June 1, 2018, just over 3,200 women were serving sentences, including about 2,550 in custody and 620 under electronic surveillance (an ankle monitor). This figure has doubled since 1986, but their proportion within the prison population (less than 4 percent) has nevertheless changed very little. Canada and France are no different than the majority of

Western countries, where often less than 5 percent of incarcerated people are women. Why do so few women face criminal prosecution? Do they commit fewer offenses, or are they charged and convicted less often than men?

Are Women Less Criminal?

Criminology has long viewed women as harmless. The field maintains that women commit fewer illegal acts, that they resort to violence (especially interpersonal violence) less often than men, and thus that the offenses they commit bring less harm to society than those committed by men. The research carried out on this subject has been based on an essentialist[2] vision of women and a strong methodological bias: only what is sought is found. The research of Vanessa R. Panfil on young queer and gay people affiliated with gangs in the United States clearly reveals this bias.[3] She shows that previous researchers deemed that there were no gay people in gangs because the heterosexuality of gang members was taken as a given.

The various ways that the violence of women has been obscured has contributed to the obscuring of their criminality.[4] It is nevertheless true that women engage less, or differently, in criminal activities than men, because of their socialization or lack of criminal opportunities. Freda Adler proffered this hypothesis in a milestone book, *Sisters in Crime*,[5] in which she maintains that progress toward the equality of the sexes also means greater access to criminal activity for women, white-collar crime in particular.

Are Women Punished Less?

The theory that the judicial system is more hostile to men has no basis in fact (see chapter 2). So how can the criminal justice system's treatment of women be described? A hypothesis that was long maintained was that posited by Otto Pollak describing the "chivalrous" treatment of female offenders.[6] This expression designates the leniency with which women are supposedly treated throughout criminal proceedings: they are arrested less, charged less, and convicted less often than men, and when they are convicted, they are given less severe sentences than men. According to this hypothesis, women thus receive an "unexpected benefit of patriarchy" that allows them to partly avoid criminal liability and receive less severe punishments.

The notion of "chivalrous" treatment of female offenders has been thoroughly debated,[7] and some research supports the inverse hypothesis, the "evil woman" hypothesis, according to which women are sentenced more severely than men precisely because they do not conform to gender norms.

The Criminalization of Women and Forms of Social Control

Women's history is marked by forms of criminalization and punishment specific to them, generally pertaining to their rights over their bodies, including access to abortion[8] or their sexuality (for example, the *tondues* during Liberation in France or the criminalization of sex work).

But above all, the forms of social control are also applied to women outside the criminal justice system.[9] Indeed, feminist works have highlighted other forms of control to which women are subjected, in particular in the domestic sphere, through family law (for example, child custody law), social policies, or within medical and psychiatric institutions. These works have also shown that the maternal role has an absolute reference value which, much like femininity, factors into how the deviance of women is evaluated.[10]

Incarcerated Women: A Group Portrait

It's not enough to have committed an offense to be criminalized, as chapter 2 showed. Rare are those who have never committed the slightest offense.[11] Consequently, committing an offense is necessary, but not sufficient, to be criminalized.[12] In many respects, incarcerated women are no different from the rest of the prison population: they belong overwhelmingly to the working class, are often children of immigration and colonial history, their level of education is inferior to that of the rest of the population, and many among them use drugs or suffer from psychological issues. In other words, the characteristics of the most precarious populations. This explains the significant proportion of incarcerated women who are involved in sex work—a phenomenon that, in Canada and in France, cannot be solely explained by the criminalization of offering sexual services.[13]

Beyond this overview, research has revealed greater insight into the specific criminal trajectories of women.[14] I will more closely examine how the paths of incarcerated women are determined by race and citizenship on the one hand, and by sexual and physical victimhood on the other. I will then explain how certain women are criminalized "by association," and why lesbians and trans women are overrepresented among incarcerated women.

Racialization and Criminalization

The prohibition in France of ethnic statistics makes it difficult to closely evaluate the ways in which people of color are criminalized, unlike other countries such as Canada or the United States. There is, however, no doubt about the overcriminalization of people of color. Various factors contribute to this phenomenon: the definition of offenses (for example, the criminalization of using a product specific to an ethnic minority), police work (what is called "racial profiling" in Canada and *contrôles au faciès* in France), and sentencing. Arthur Vuattoux's research has demonstrated how Romani girls in France do not benefit from the gendered judicial treatment generally reserved for non-Romani girls, and that they are thus more harshly sentenced than white girls.[15]

But the ways in which racialization shapes criminalization doesn't begin with an encounter with the criminal justice system. In the United States, the expression "school-to-prison pipeline" describes the long process that leads youth belonging to an ethnic minority to prison: the toughening of disciplinary practices within educational institutions and their increased reliance on police leads to the exclusion of non-white youth from the school system, and their itinerancy and periodic homelessness can lead to prison. This phenomenon can also be observed among LGBTQ youth (see below) and people with disabilities.

Racialization also plays a role in how one's sentence is served. Indigenous women in Canada make up the most overrepresented group in prison: although Indigenous people make up only 4 percent of the general population, Indigenous women represent 43 percent of women in prison.[16] In addition to these prison population statistics, these women live/endure their sentences differently. As pointed out by the Canadian feminist Karlene Faith, "these women serve longer sentences, not because of the severity of their crime, but because they cannot adapt to the prisons of their colonizers."[17]

Criminal Paths and Physical and Sexual Victimhood

The research conducted on the criminal paths of incarcerated women has long highlighted the ways in which they are subjected to sexual and physical victimhood.[18] Surveys conducted in the United States estimate that between 30 percent and 80 percent of incarcerated female minors have been victims of sexual abuse, often at a very young age.[19] Despite the range in their estimations, these surveys all indicate that the proportion of people who have been victims of sexual violence is much higher in prisons for women than in prisons for men. Sexual victimhood is thus one of the most predictive variables for criminalization.

In some US research, the expression "sexual-abuse-to-prison pipeline" conveys this phenomenon specific to the experiences of criminalized women.[20] It designates the process that leads female victims of sexual abuse to become incarcerated. This machine is set into motion when girls or young women run away to escape sexual (or physical) harm that often takes place in the home. Their financial and emotional precarity then severely exposes them to the risk of incarceration. But time in prison reinforces their trauma, and when they leave, their heightened vulnerability puts them at increased risk of being victims once again.

A very similar phenomenon explains the significant proportion of incarcerated women who were victims of domestic violence (chapter 2 explored the particular case of those in prison for self-defense). There are no statistics for France or Canada, but there is no reason to think that the situation would be any different than that of other Western countries. According to a study conducted by the British charitable association Prison Reform Trust, between 50 percent and 75 percent of incarcerated women in the United Kingdom have been victims of domestic violence.[21] This same study describes the "vicious cycle" of victimization and the committing of offenses that women find themselves in. They are wary of the legal system, from which they have never received aid, and they can find themselves in even greater precariousness, and often homelessness, because of the scant resources made available to female victims.

Lesbians and Trans Women

Although there is no scientific consensus on the proportion of LGBTQ people among perpetrators of crimes, there is no question that lesbians and trans women are overrepresented in prison. Studies in Canada and France are still in their early days, but a few American studies are rather indicative. One study estimates that 13 percent to 15 percent of minors who encounter the judicial system are LGBTQ people, while it is estimated that their proportion in the prison population is between 5 percent to 7 percent.[22] A more recent study estimates that the rate of incarceration of people who identify as lesbians, homosexual, or bisexual is three times higher than that of the rest of the population.[23]

This phenomenon is certainly not unrelated from biases that guide judicial decisions. For example, the stereotype of the "aggressive lesbian," whose socio-historical construction has been examined by Estelle Freedman,[24] contributes to the greater risk for lesbians in the United States of being sentenced to capital punishment, as compared to heterosexual women convicted of similar offenses.[25] The overrepresentation of LGBTQ people among incarcerated women is likely also explained by the presence of certain risk factors (broken families, difficulty finding work, fragility of social resources, etc.) and different forms of vulnerability (drug abuse, various high-risk behaviors, etc.) that they experience to a considerable degree and which also play a role in the criminal paths of the general population, as suggested by Charlotte Knight and Kath Wilson.[26] These two authors also point out that the phenomenon of the school-to-prison pipeline, previously mentioned regarding people of color, also affects LGBTQ people due to behaviors they adopt to avoid homophobic or transphobic attacks, and which lead to their exclusion from the school system. Impacted by mental health problems, familial conflicts, and vagrancy, LGBTQ youth have criminal paths very similar to those of ethnic minority youth.

Criminal by Association

In the United States in the 1990s, media coverage of Kemba Smith's case and the protests in her support highlighted the ways in which women are criminalized through their intimate relations with men. Kemba Smith was seven months pregnant when she was arrested. After four years in an abusive relationship, she had participated in certain criminal activities with her partner, who was involved in drug trafficking. The policy of mandatory minimum sentences did not allow for the circumstances of these activities to be taken into account, and in 1994 Kemba Smith was sentenced to more than twenty years in prison.[27]

Kemba Smith's case is not an isolated one. A study done in the United Kingdom shows that 48 percent of incarcerated women who are drug users committed an offense to help a friend or family member who was also a drug user, which is the case for only 22 percent of incarcerated men.[28] These figures show how the altruism and devotion toward their relatives (in particular, for their children) and friends is a leading motivation for women to engage in criminal activities. Furthermore, women act alone less often than men, especially in the case of extremely serious crimes, and women who commit a crime often do it with the help of a man, without whom they would perhaps never have done so. Whether defending themselves from men, acting alongside them, or committing an offense in service of them, women often engage in criminal acts because of men—though this does not negate their own responsibility.

Women's criminalization by association takes a variety of forms. Some ancillary tasks (such as accounting or money laundering) performed by women whose partners are engaged in criminal activities or belong to criminal organizations can be equated by them to domestic work, especially because they are not compensated for it. Their criminalization by association also results from sexual or physical harm inflicted on children, whether women are the accomplices of men (usually their partners) or fall short of their duty to protect. When these women are arrested, the potentially abusive nature of the relationships is rarely taken into consideration. In the United States legal system, their loyalty (if they refuse to testify against their partner) can procure them an even harsher sentence.

Criminalization by association shows the gendered division of criminal work, with drug trafficking as an edifying example. Women generally handle the least lucrative tasks, in particular the sale of drugs, which specially exposes them to arrest and to harassment by their clientele. They also overwhelmingly handle the often international transport of merchandise,[29] another task indispensable to trafficking, which incurs the risk of being imprisoned far from their support networks. Women are often tasked with such roles because it is thought that they attract less attention, and because their anatomy generally allows for the concealment of products. They frequently accept these risks to provide for their families (usually their children) in the absence of other opportunities, and because they are often coerced into doing so by manipulative men involved in these activities.[30]

Women's Sentences

Marilyn Buck[31] compared the life of women in prison to the life of women with an "abusive partner."[32] Indeed, all aspects of their private lives are controlled in both scenarios. For example, incarcerated women, much like incarcerated men, are often subjected to regular strip searches, which can be intrusive or even abusive. In France as in Canada, in prisons for women, strip searches are systematically performed by female guards, but trans women incarcerated in prisons for men are searched by male guards.[33] Their sexuality is also controlled. This plays out differently in prisons for women and in prisons for men, and whether the person incarcerated is heterosexual or homosexual. Prisons for men are more tolerant of hetero-sexual acts under the pretext of the supposed naturalness of men's "sexual needs." Prisons for women are more tolerant of homosexual relationships, likely because they are often equated to mere friendships.

With equivalent sentence lengths and prison conditions, the social and personal consequences (including those on physi-cal and mental health) of incarceration are more significant for women than for men.[34] Women are more stigmatized for serving time in prison than men. They find themselves more isolated, because prisons for women are far less numerous than those for men[35] and so they are often incarcerated in cor-rectional institutions far from their relatives and loved ones.

As with other hardships (for example, serious illness), women in prison find themselves more alone than men. Men are more likely to leave women who are incarcerated than women are to abandon their incarcerated partners or spouses. Additionally, women who are incarcerated or who have been incarcerated have less chance of finding a partner than men in similar situ-ations. The support that women receive comes primarily from other women. Furthermore, when women are incarcerated, their children are put at even greater risk for being placed in custody in an institution or with people outside of their family than is the case when men are incarcerated.

Paradoxically, for the most vulnerable people, prison can turn out to be a place where they feel safe, supported, and heard —it can even be a place of solidarity among women. Some speak of their incarceration as a moment of "recovery," espe-cially if they had previously been living on the street, using drugs, or were victims of violence at the hands of men. These "unexpected benefits" of incarceration highlight the absurdity of the system: these women gain access to certain resources *inside* that they lack on the *outside*, access that would in fact have allowed them to avoid incarceration in the first place. For certain women, another unexpected benefit of incarceration is involvement in a lesbian relationship, which is often described in a very positive manner—especially as compared to their previous heterosexual relationships.[36]

I will now delve deeper into the impact of incarceration on two more specific categories of women: mothers and trans women.

Mothers in Prison

While incarcerated men can generally count on the mother of their child (or their own mother or sister) to take care of their children and bring them to the visiting rooms in the prison, incarcerated women must often count on other women rather than their male partners.[37] For this reason, incarcerated mothers are at greater risk of their children being placed in foster care and losing their right to custody than incarcerated fathers.

Many prison systems grant accommodations to pregnant women and to mothers of young children: for example, the mother-child program in federal prisons in Canada, which allows children to stay with their mother until the age of four, or, in France, in mother-child units (or nurseries) for incarcerated women with children under eighteen months. Children are extremely valued in prisons for women because their presence allows mothers to demonstrate qualities seen as typically feminine (gentleness, kindness, etc.).[38] This goes hand in hand with the stigmatization of women who committed infanticide.

Trans Women in Prison

The particularly harsh nature of sentences served by trans women has been brought to the public's attention in recent years thanks to the media coverage in the United States of the cases of CeCe McDonald (see insert on p. 48) and Chelsea Manning, a whistleblower incarcerated from 2010 to 2017, then once again in 2019, as part of the WikiLeaks affair. The character Sophia Burset, a young trans woman played by Laverne Cox in the television series *Orange Is the New Black,* has also helped to shine a light on the experience of trans women behind bars. For these women, incarceration has severe consequences on their health, social life, and more—much more than is the case for the rest of the prison population, all things being otherwise equal.

Like intersex people, trans women are especially impacted by the sex segregation within the prison system (prisons "for men" versus "for women"), which is based on the civil status and appearance of the genitalia of those in question. Trans women are thus frequently incarcerated in prisons for men. This type of housing allocation, which does not respect these women's lived identity, is detrimental to their health, especially their psychological health, because they are unable to dress in a way that conforms to their gender (due to the prohibition of certain clothing) or access certain hygiene and maintenance products (such as makeup).[39] On the other hand, placing trans people in separate units, with the aim of protecting and/or "pinkwashing" (see chapter 5) creates a great deal of problems, since it can increase their social isolation and their risk of victimhood.[40] A notable exception is federal prisons in Canada, which have granted trans people the right to choose the type of institution they will be incarcerated in since 2017.

Despite a copious amount of literature showing that the prohibition or restriction to access to hormone treatments and to reconstructive surgery (also known as gender affirmation surgery) violates the rights of trans people, numerous prisons refuse them access to this type of care or to aftercare, especially if they have not already begun these medical procedures on the outside (and in official care settings).[41] The deprivation of hormone treatments has physiological effects (fatigue, headaches, sleep problems, etc.) in addition to a psychological impact.

Incarcerated trans women also face a greater risk for sexual harm at the hands of their fellow prisoners or by members of the prison staff. In Canada as in France, this risk, which has been well documented by community organizations, is difficult to evaluate.[42] One of the rare quantitative studies done in the United States on this subject revealed that trans people experience thirteen times more sexual violence than the rest of the prison population.[43] The idea that this kind of violence does not exist in France was disproven by the conviction of three prison guards in 1999 (upheld on appeal the following year) for sexual assaults committed against trans people in solitary confinement in the jail for men in Fleury-Mérogis in 1995–6.[44] Even if the scope of this violence is difficult to quantify, fear still greatly shapes the experience of trans people in prison, as well as in their encounters with the police.

Prisons for Women and the Treatment of Incarcerated Women

Certain currents of feminism claim that men and women should be treated strictly in the same way, while other currents (such as differentialist feminism) call for "equality in difference," meaning that they believe equality can be achieved through differential treatment (for example, affirmative action). In the debate surrounding prisons, the question is whether or not there should be a demand that incarcerated women receive the same treatment as incarcerated men.

An Institution Conceived for Men

French law lays out few specific accommodations for incarcerated women. It does not take a woman's status as a mother into account when making decisions about disciplinary decisions, such as sending women to "the hole" (as other judicial systems do), and the only accommodations relating to women in the Code of Criminal Procedure concern pregnancy (article D399 *et seq.*). Furthermore, as the sociologist Corinne Rostaing observes, "nothing allows for differential treatment of the two sexes in the eighty-six articles of the 2009 law."[45] Corinne Rostaing also points out that the word "woman" only appears in two articles, both relating to medical treatment.

Nevertheless, the existence of mother-child units and policies regarding female staff in prisons for women in France illustrates what the sociologist Coline Cardi shows in her research: when correctional institutions think of women, it is above all as (future) mothers.[46] In certain cases, it is about avoiding pregnancy at all costs; in others it is to preserve the "unique" and wonderful bond between mother and child. This analysis is far from limited to France. It is manifested, in a variety of ways, in feminist activist and criminologist denunciations of prison as an institution created by men for other men, and where women are treated just as women are treated elsewhere within patriarchal society.

This treatment has been widely denounced in feminist scholarship and movements. In the 1970s, for example, there were protests against sexual abuse suffered by incarcerated women, as in the case of Joan Little (see insert on p. 69). Another issue of concern is the way that domesticity is maintained in prison. One example of the infantilizing manner in which incarcerated women are often treated is the systematic use of maiden names for those who have taken their spouse's name prior to incarceration. Another is that the professional development courses and activities that are offered to women generally reduce them to the role of assistant, housewife, spouse, and/or mother by focusing on secretarial and aesthetician work, cooking, sewing, etc. Furthermore, the prevalence of psychoactive drugs in prisons for women (much higher than in prisons for men) demonstrates the high level of attention paid to their behavior during their treatment—or, in other words, their domestication.

In the 1966 book *Society of Women*, Rose Giallombardo examined the different forms of treatment men and women receive from the criminal justice system, in particular when it comes to rehabilitation.[47] As Dvora Groman and Claude Gaugeron note, "The role of women is perpetuated even behind bars; 'resocialization' has, for the detainee, a simple meaning: certain standards of morality (especially sexual) must be instilled in her and she must be prepared to resume her role as mother of the family in society."[48] This characterization remains true in many prisons for women around the world.

Joan Little (born 1953)

In August 1974, a twenty-one-year-old African-American woman named Joan Little killed a white guard who was trying to sexually assault her, then escaped from a North Carolina jail. Arrested not long after, she was tried and sentenced to death.

Her case quickly drew the attention of the media, and protests were organized to support her. She was supported by organizations rooted in feminist movements, African-American liberation movements, and movements for the abolition of the death penalty. Among her most famous supporters was the civil rights activist Rosa Parks, who established a support committee for Joan Little in Detroit. Angela Davis (see insert on p. 24), involved in the defense of Joan Little, wrote a still-renowned article about her: "Joan Little: The Dialectics of Rape,"[49] in which she describes the way in which the victimhood of African-American women is constructed by both racism and sexism.

Joan Little was ultimately acquitted in August 1975.

Treat Women Like Men?

Prisons for women have long had the reputation of being, on the whole, less strict than prisons for men, mainly because of the rarity of escapes and riots. Meda Chesney-Lind has observed, however, that beginning in the 1990s in the United States, there was an increasing alignment of the rules of prisons for women with those for men.[50] What she describes as a "vengeful equity" translated, for women, to harsher prison conditions (for example, when they are hospitalized to give birth). But at the turn of the twenty-first century, an inverse movement emerged as prisons in North America began to develop "gender mainstreaming" approaches. These aim to provide an "environment that reflects an understanding of the realities of women's lives and addresses the issues of women."[51] In practical terms, these "gender-responsive"[52] approaches led to the establishment of programs intended to respond to the specific needs of women, especially drug use, sexual trauma, and the maintenance of parental and familial relations.[53] Some correctional institutions are conceived entirely around this approach[54] and even call themselves "women-centered prisons."[55]

The Trap of Gender Mainstreaming

Gendered approaches are partially the result of campaigns in favor of improved prison conditions for women. But, as Brady T. Heine and Sarah K. Tyson have documented, these approaches are generally fueled by the broader anti-violence movements begun by feminists in the 1970s.[56] Gendered approaches first appeared in Canada after the publication of a report titled *La création de choix* (Creating Choices), which formulated propositions for reforms to the ways prisons treat women (new types of establishments, programs specifically for women, etc.).[57] In the United States, as noted by Jodie M. Lawston and Erica R. Meiners in the course of their research, one of the first examples of this type of approach was the proposal, made in 2006 by California's then-governor Arnold Schwarzenegger, to transfer 4,500 women convicted of nonviolent crimes to "community correctional facilities" created "specifically" to respond to the needs of women.[58] These transferred women would have freed up additional space for incarcerated men.[59]

Certain feminists have fiercely criticized these gendered approaches, mainly because the proposed programs are based on essentialist visions of the needs of women.[60] Julia Sudbury highlighted this aspect in pointing out that these approaches presuppose that only women are incarcerated in "prisons for women,"[61] a presupposition that excludes trans men and nonbinary people detained in these correctional institutions. Their experiences are thus ignored, as are those of trans women incarcerated in "prisons for men."

Furthermore, as Rose Braz explains, prison cannot create an environment that responds to the needs of women; prison cannot address the problems of women because it creates them.[62] If the goal is to stop incarcerating women, then social inequalities, racism, and the patriarchy must be tackled instead of giving incarcerated women access to resources, especially since there is no evidence that this approach actually works. This gendered approach thus creates the justification for the construction of new prisons and actually participates, often under the guise of progressiveness, in the further expansion of the criminal justice system.[63] As Jodie M. Lawston and Erica R. Meiners write quite accurately, gender mainstreaming "participate[s] in redrawing the boundaries of, and potentially expanding, the carceral state."[64]

These prisons also point to an impasse of identity politics that focus on the recognition of certain traits or life histories that can be perfectly incorporated by the state and prison policies. They also rely on an essentially reformist feminism, profoundly inspired by carceral feminism (see chapter 5). Additionally, as Jodie M. Lawston and Erica R. Meiners point out, criticism is equally warranted for gender mainstreaming approaches to prison policies that intend to take the specific needs of LGBTQ people into account.[65] Chapter 5 explores the objections that queer abolitionism has to this approach.

4

The Women at the Prison Gates

This chapter describes the various experiences of women who have relatives and loved ones in prison, and the ways they are affected by the existence of prison. But should this examination be limited to those experiences? How can the sentences each woman serves be described, by each in her own way? How does this form of sentence affect their lives? The reflections below are based in large part on my research[1] and my own experience —which might also explain some of the deficiencies. For example, the experiences of homosexual couples, families with same-sex parents, and undocumented people coping with prison sentences would merit their own explorations. The resources available at the time of writing are unfortunately insufficient to do more than mention these important experiences briefly.

The Invisible Woman

Is it possible to recall the name of just one of these women? If anyone is remembered, it is generally because of their partner or their son, and often because the woman helped them escape or because they were their best defenders. In France, books by Serge Livrozet and Georges Courtois are among the typical recommendations for those interested in critiques of prison. But what about their partners?[2] Compared with the books written by prisoners and ex-prisoners, those written by their relatives are far less common. Several publishing houses do regularly publish testimonies by prisoners' partners (and sometimes mothers), but they are rather uninteresting and slightly voyeur-istic.[3] So, how many women are there who have incarcerated relatives and loved ones (who are usually, though not always, male),[4] and how should they be referred to?

"Families" and "Relatives and Friends"

In France, at the beginning of the 2000s, the Institut national de la statistique et des études économiques (INSEE) estimated that the spouses, parents, siblings, children, and grandchildren of incarcerated people represent 320,000 adults and 63,200 minors.[5] A 2007 Canadian study estimated that 357,604 children saw their fathers incarcerated each year.[6] Thus each year, there are roughly a half-million people in France affected by the imprisonment of a relative. In prison jargon, these people are often identified using the term "family."

This denomination is problematic because what might be colloquially understood as "family" does not always corre-spond to an administrative definition. Black feminists, notably Patricia Hills Collins, have emphasized the importance of the tradition of "othermothers"[7] for African Americans.[8] The term "family" thus poorly captures the network of solidarity and care that can surround prisoners, in particular women. Indeed, support from one's family can in some cases be less common than support from friends or from brothers and sisters in misery (former fellow prisoners or fellow sex workers, etc.). LGBTQ people, for example, often count on other LGBTQ people, identified by the anglophone expression "chosen family." The association Black and Pink (see insert on p. 75) responds to this need by helping incarcerated LGBTQ people construct solidar-ity networks outside of their biological families. For all these reasons, I prefer the term "relatives and friends," which places less emphasis on belonging to a family than on the people who show some form of solidarity, whether it is material, financial, or emotional.

Black and Pink (United States)

Black and Pink is an LGBTQ abolitionist and community building organization founded in Boston in 2004 by Jason Lydon, a Unitarian church pastor, who served as director until 2017.

Black and Pink supports LGBTQ people and those with HIV who are in prison. Its members maintain correspondence with prisoners, inform them of their rights, and accompany them throughout their legal proceedings.

In 2010 Black and Pink began publishing a journal entitled *Black and Pink News*, distributed to 13,000 people in prison.

Black and Pink also undertakes political campaigns to denounce the situation of LGBTQ people and those with HIV in prison, and also regularly publishes research on the subject.

An organization very similar to Black and Pink, Bent Bars, was established in the United Kingdom in 2009.

Chapter 3 explored how solidarity (sending money, visiting, etc.) is more common for men in prison than for women. Although prisons, for the most part, incarcerate men, solidarity is generally carried out by women. There is nothing mysterious about it: it is the expected societal role for women (particularly mothers and wives), and taking care of others is often thought of as a "naturally" feminine quality. Solidarity, however, is sometimes a burden for women (see chapter 6).

Forms of Invisibility

There are many forms of invisibility that relatives and friends of incarcerated people endure. This group has represented a blind spot in research fields, especially in the sociology of the family and of the prison. This has begun to change in France,[9] but only as recently as the early 2000s. Meanwhile, the Canadian journal *Criminology* dedicated a 2019 issue to the "relatives and friends of criminalized people," signaling the emergence of a new field of research.[10] It is still surprising, however, that these people have remained in the shadows for so long, especially since it is a matter of "common sense" that family—whether dissociated, blended, absent, broken, or dysfunctional—has always been the primary factor for delinquency.

The relatives and friends of incarcerated people are also largely ignored by public policies. This might be surprising, too, because in terms of preventing delinquency and fighting recidivism, the quality of social bonds is generally considered a determining factor. There are also questions concerning the lack of support for the relatives and friends of incarcerated people by family policies, which increasingly claim to be motivated by the notion that society must "help the helpers." Suffering also exists among children whose parents are in prison, caused by absence, stigmatization, and even guilt. This collective negligence on the part of public policies reflects a similar attitude within the criminal justice system, which only takes an interest in the relatives and friends of the criminalized individuals during sentencing and release procedures (see below).

The invisibility that relatives and friends of incarcerated people suffer from is also evident in media coverage of prisons. There are sometimes reports on protests organized by relatives and friends, which often take place in front of prisons after a death inside the prison, or in reaction to a strike by prison staff that prevents visits. These events are rare enough for the media to consider them newsworthy. When the media discusses prison, however, they tend to focus more on the people who live *off of* it (the prison staff and the social workers,[11] the "experts," and the nonprofit organizations) than on those who *live it* (incarcerated people and, in their own way, their relatives and friends). Furthermore, they often concentrate on the workplace suffering of prison staff, or on the general state of prisons. The scarcity of debates on the social function of prison, and on the difficulty that those who *live it* have in accessing the public discourse, also inspired me to begin my doctoral studies in 2000. That year in France, prison was the subject of numerous political and media debates, all following the publication of Dr. Véronique Vasseur's voyeuristic and sensationalist book detailing her work at the La Santé jail in Paris, but which primarily focused on her "adventures" there. Despite the place that prison occupied in the public sphere, and the near-unanimity in denouncing the shameful conditions in which people are confined, no real changes were made. The episode also emphasized the monopoly position that legitimists have in public debates on prisons, as well as the systematic exclusion of the people who are most impacted by the existence of the prison system.

The invisibility of the relatives and friends of incarcerated people is also political—notably in abolitionist movements (see chapter 5). Collectives of relatives and friends of incarcerated people are rare.[12] Those in Canada are primarily based on mutual aid, such as Mothers Offering Mutual Support (MOMS). Apart from groups made up of relatives and comrades of political prisoners (such as exist among Basque and Corsican national liberation fighters in France), these collectives are also generally ephemeral, and it is rare that they lead to political scrutiny or formulated demands. These collectives are hampered by the difficulty of mobilizing people whose experience with prison is frequently marked by shame (regardless of the offense that resulted in the incarceration of their loved one) and sometimes even by secrecy. Thus, these collectives often struggle to organize beyond networks that act strictly as affinity groups, or to free themselves from prison hierarchies (see chapter 6). Collectives of relatives and friends of victims of state crimes, despite facing difficulties of different kinds, are often the ones to succeed in sustaining their activities. For example, in France, there is the Association des familles en lutte contre l'insécurité et les décès en détention (AFLIDD, Association of Families Fighting Against Insecurity and Death in Custody), which is related to the Mouvement immigration banlieue (MIB, Suburbs Immigration Movement), created in November 1999, and to the group Justice for Adama Traore, to cite a more recent example.

Material, Financial, and Emotional Costs

Maintaining a relationship with an incarcerated person happens primarily through visits, written correspondence, and phone calls. These forms of relationship maintenance require certain types of skills: for example, the ability to write correspondence to the facilities holding the incarcerated person, as well as the criminal and correctional administrations. In addition, status as an entrepreneur or white-collar professional allows more availability for visits. For a large portion of incarcerated people and their relatives and friends, who sometimes have difficulty with writing and/or with the dominant language of the prison officials, visits are the preferred way of maintaining relationships. But obtaining a visitor permit is often described as complicated, due to the legal-administrative labyrinth and its delays, the impossibility of proving relationships that are not formalized by marriage, etc.

"Room and Board"?

People in prison are often said to be provided with "room and board" at the taxpayer's expense, an assertion that eludes the question of the costs of imprisonment. It is generally estimated that the costs of maintaining a decent lifestyle for a detained person is between $115 and $175 US per month. This includes renting a television, buying hygiene products (toothbrush, soap, etc.) and other products such as cigarettes, which are typically necessary within prison social life. But the price of the products sold in prison is often much higher than prices on the outside.

Because of the scarcity of prison work and its scant payment, these costs are generally shouldered by relatives and friends, who often see a decrease in resources available for their own homes as a result. There are also new expenses incurred— lawyer fees and the cost of visits primarily, but also, in some cases, payments to victims, who might later serve as positive character references during early-release proceedings. In a French study that is already outdated, the Centre de recherche pour l'étude et l'observation des conditions de vie (CREDOC, Research Center for the Study and Observation of Living Conditions) estimated that, on average, relatives and friends spend roughly $230 each month for an incarcerated person. The same 2000 study noted that 53 percent of these relatives and friends earned less than $1,050 per month, making them part of the poorest segment of the population. And they are often required to change jobs to be able to support their incarcerated relative, friend, or loved one.[13] Given the age of the study, that cost is likely even higher now.

One of the most significant expenses for relatives and friends is visiting prison. Their costs are calculated based not only on the distance and form of transportation, but also on the time off from other work that travel and visits require: the average roundtrip travel time to the prison is often three times longer than the visit itself. People are frequently incarcerated far from their relatives and friends, and regularly transferred between prisons, which administrators justify as a matter of security, leading to the greater travel expenses. In France it is estimated to cost $30 per visit to jails and $45 to prisons.[14] Unfortunately, there are still too few quantitative studies to be able to precisely describe the broader circumstances (for example, in Canada), but qualitative studies conducted in many countries largely point to significant financial expenses being shouldered by relatives and friends. These expenses will only increase with the ubiquitous trend of building prisons farther and farther from cities.

The Emotional Costs

Incarceration, for a loved one, is generally described as something similar to the "prison shock" that prisoners experience, which is not unlike a state of paralysis. As with any serious event, incarceration acts as a "litmus test." Although it sometimes allows for the expression of sentiments that might be difficult to express in normal situations, it is a powerful contributor to social and family breakdowns. More than 10 percent of partnerships are broken during the first month of incarceration, and 20 percent during the first year. And several "short" sentences can lead to comparable results.[15]

Even if the incarceration of a loved one sometimes becomes its own routine, relatives and friends of incarcerated people often exhibit a sense of shame, since they are considered (or consider themselves) guilty by association. In addition to shame there is often concern (for the safety of their loved one, about the company they keep, about their living conditions in prison), as well as a feeling of powerlessness. Sadness and anxiety can manifest in physical symptoms (depression, poor mood, etc.).[16] Many relatives and friends say that they have faced hostility, suspicion, and ridicule. Many women say that have been insulted by passersby as they waited in front of a prison. The relatives and friends of incarcerated people can suffer from "stigma by association,"[17] to borrow an expression from US sociologist Erving Goffman, and feel that they have become pariahs. The self-fulfilling prophecy effect of this stigma then engenders a feeling of vulnerability.

Relatives and friends of prisoners often speak about facing disapproval within their own families. Some spouses are encouraged to divorce, notably by their parents. Relationships with in-laws can become hostile, especially when incarceration itself is blamed on the spouse. Forms of solidarity (visits, laundry, sending money, etc.) can become litigious subjects between different members of the larger family. And fear of gossip (for example, if someone does not appear "affected" enough) brings about a greater social isolation, turning women into "prisoners" in their own homes. Furthermore, like many dramatic events, the incarceration of a loved one tends to distance relatives and friends from community members, who often do not know how to discuss the matter. Relatives and friends of incarcerated people often describe social networks that shrink to the few people with whom they share similar experiences.

Concealing the fact of an incarcerated loved one is relatively common, sometimes even within a family (in particular, in privileged social milieus). Some people move to avoid the judgment of their neighbors, especially in small towns. On official documents, some report their relatives and friends as "deceased," rather than reporting their incarceration. This further perpetuates a form of "civil death," meaning the erosion of civic, civil, and family rights. It is very telling that most social institutions do not include incarcerated people when allocating state assistance based on numbers of household members.

The Social Costs of Incarceration

Since prison affects more than just incarcerated people, how can its social costs be calculated? Finding an answer to this question requires a reexamination of the social function of prison.

Family Faced with Imprisonment

The incarceration of a person often upsets the family balance. Fathers, for example, due to the lack of work in prison as well as its meager pay, lament that they are removed from their traditional role as a breadwinner. In the event of divorce, the

exercise of parental authority and visitation rights are complicated. Even though there are "bébés parloir" (children born
from visits, more common outside the US), there is a prohibition on medically assisted procreation for prisoners. And in
adoption proceedings, couples in which one partner is incarcerated are usually disqualified. The result is that many couples,
and especially women (whether incarcerated or the partner of
a prisoner), are prevented from having children.

The relatives and friends of incarcerated people are often
unable to maintain relationships with them, and even find
that communication comes to a stop. Indeed, breakups initi-
ated by prisoners are common. Severing a relationship is one
way of protecting oneself from the worst kind of separation
(abandonment) or protecting one's relatives and friends, even
if what they claim might not be entirely true: "I'd rather my
relatives and friends not come to see me, I want to spare them."
For those incarcerated, the clash between *outside* and *inside*
identities, put on display in the visiting room, under the gaze of
fellow prisoners and guards, is sometimes a source of anxiety.
Willful and permanent attacks on intimacy, which challenge
the autonomy of the person and their capacity to interact with
others (through the various constraints on relationships with
their relatives and friends), can also elicit self-protective actions
(preferring not to see their relatives and friends rather than be
subjected to these constraints).

Doing one's "time" *inside* and maintaining prior relationships
outside is often thought to be incompatible. This phenomenon,
described by the sociological expressions "prison socialization"
and "prisonization," results in feelings of estrangement. Thus,
prisoners and their relatives and friends often discuss the fact
that communication between *inside* and *outside* can become,
over time, strained. Conversations themselves become increasingly superficial—as is often seen with seriously ill people.

Secondary Victims?

The many effects of incarceration on relatives and friends are impossible to fully detail, but it is nevertheless important to emphasize that release from prison does not mark the end of the "sentence" for relatives and friends. The release procedure is often accompanied by a significant mental toll for women, and the people who are released from prison often need various forms of care, generally fulfilled by women. Furthermore, the effects of incarceration (on intimacy, sexuality, etc.) are generally long-lasting, and relatives and friends often say that release from prison causes a disruption very similar to the one caused by incarceration.

Any discussion of the effects of incarceration on relatives and friends must include a focus on children whose parents are incarcerated. The separation created is a source of suffering, but it is important to point out that, similar to other family events (like a divorce, a serious illness, or death), incarceration itself has no specific effects on the children;[18] the resulting effects depend on the familial, social, and individual resources that the children and their families possess. The term "second-generation prisoners," often used in the United States, reveals a phenomenon that also exists elsewhere: prisoners often had a loved one, usually a father, who was incarcerated. But make no mistake: the risk of being incarcerated depends primarily on social factors, and so this phenomenon points to the fact that social inequalities are generational. Incarcerated men are not bad fathers, nor does the absence of the father from the family home result in greater risk of incarceration for children later in life.

Various expressions have been used to designate the ways in which people are affected by the incarceration of a loved one, such as "the other sentence."[19] But the negative impacts of a sentence on people who are not themselves convicted leads to questions surrounding the legality of a criminal justice system that also punishes innocent people, in violation of the principle of the individual nature of penalties (the principle according to which the sentence must be specific to the person who receives it): the relatives and friends of prisoners, especially their children, are the secondary victims of incarceration.

It's important to revisit the "social costs" of the criminal justice system, as investigated by Alvaro Pires, Piere Landreville, and Victor Blankevoort.[20] If the relatives and friends of prisoners can be considered "secondary" victims, it is because, as they claim, "the real ideological-political target of the criminal justice system is the families more than the individuals." This observation is especially interesting because it evokes questions about the social function of prison itself. Prison is, perhaps, less designed to affect those on the *inside* than those on the *outside*. Émile Durkheim has drawn attention to the vengeful nature of sentencing, the goal of which is not to rehabilitate offenders, but to remind others of the law, and by doing so revitalize the "collective conscience."[21]

The Relatives and Friends of Incarcerated People: Profit Streams

In the United States, the services offered to relatives and friends (such as phone calls, video calls, text messages, or sending money to incarcerated people) constitute a growing economic sector, and one of the main providers is JPay (see insert on p. 85). In France, this sector is still underdeveloped, often limited to organizations that, under the pretext of philanthropy, offer hospitality services, housing, and even visitation assistance.

Incite! and other activist groups in the United States have criticized the emergence of this sector, which they call the "nonprofit industrial complex."[22] Its development, which is of course not completely separate from the prison-industrial complex (see chapter 1), nor from the expansion of the institutionalization and professionalization of aid, has had a far-reaching impact. Relatives and friends of incarcerated people (the other populations it "serves") have been turned into an "economic niche," and there is thus great financial interest

---

JPay (United States)

JPay is a private company founded in 2002 and now active in 35 of the 50 states in the United States. Its services are accessible to nearly 1.5 million incarcerated people (including some on some death row), and for those on probation or on parole.

JPay developed its services in conjunction with the introduction, in 2009, of the first tablet computer designed specifically to be used by incarcerated people. Depending on the make and model, these tablets cost between $70 and $175. Their functions are limited (it has no use outside of prisons), but, under supervision by the prison staff, they enable incarcerated people to send and receive photos, written correspondence, and audio and video messages (and even video calls). They also provide access to games, news, and educational content, as well as music. People on the outside can access these services through a website or smartphone app, from which they can send money.

The contracts that prison administrations sign with JPay cost them nothing, since JPay profits from every service that the incarcerated people and their relatives and friends pay to access. For example, sending $100 costs a user $10, 15 "stamps" (necessary to send a corresponding number of emails) cost $4.50, and a thirty-minute video call costs $9.90. Beginning in 2018, JPay contracted with the state of New York to distribute free tablets to 52,000 incarcerated people in state prisons—a contract that would bring JPay profits of more than $8.75 million by August 2020.

JPay also offers payment platforms for community correction payments and fines, which people on probation or parole must pay. It also offers, to people approaching their release from prison, the "JPay Progress Card," a prepaid debit card to be accessed upon their release.

JPay's profits total more than $46 million per year.

---

in increasing the number of criminalized people. Its development runs counter to the goals of empowerment, and to that of penal abolitionism (see chapter 6).

The Sense of Grief That Relatives and Friends Feel

From Guilt by Association to Vouching for Reintegration

The relatives and friends of prisoners are rarely taken into consideration by the criminal justice system, except during trials and release proceedings. An accused person's familial bonds, and their quality, are commonly examined during a trial, in particular for serious crimes. During public hearings, and especially in exchanges surrounding the accused person's character, there are often insinuations that their relatives might bear certain forms of responsibility for the criminal activity. Relatives of the accused, however, are rarely unaware of what's at stake during a trial, nor of the source of this temptation to "police families."[23] Mothers, partners, and wives frequently feel that they face just as much scrutiny as their relatives (whom the prosecution often attempts to portray a priori as "bad husbands" and "bad fathers"), which leads to feeling guilty by association, because they were "bad mothers," "unsupportive wives," etc.

During pre-release proceedings (which include conditional release, furlough, etc.), the family bonds of incarcerated people are examined again. In France, reports drawn up by prison social workers (CPIP), as well as sentencing judges' decisions, often allude to the role of male prisoners' partners in the process, especially within the framework of the traditional notion of being "guarantors" of their "reintegration."[24] Relatives and friends often serve as examples of positive influences. But to correspond to the image of the "woman savior" and serve as a "stabilizing force," they must be "supportive," "maternal," and "stable." They are, however, sometimes reproached for not maintaining regular contact, or for not "really" knowing their incarcerated partner, especially if they met them while they were incarcerated and thus have never lived with them on the outside.

Confronted—against their will—by the judicial and prison system, and then destabilized and stigmatized by these inter-actions, relatives and friends of prisoners are often considered both accomplices and victims.[25] They are concurrently con-fronted by two ambiguous and sometimes contradictory demands of the criminal justice system: to be responsible for the convicted person on the one hand, and then support-ive of the prisoner and act as guarantor for the ex-prisoner on the other. Analysis of institutional discourse, such as the documented narratives of relatives and friends of incarcerated people, suggests that what they feel is required of them, in the end, is less their solidarity than their penance.

From Disgrace to Resistance

Humiliation and Infantilization

Relatives and friends of incarcerated people often describe suffering caused by a lack of consideration from prison admin-istration and staff, which is especially evident in the limited information they receive concerning transfers, illnesses, and even deaths. The ignorance in which relatives and friends are kept echoes a phrase often uttered *inside*: "We know when we enter, but not when we leave ..." Staff and administrative attitudes are often received, by relatives and friends, as insults, or even punishments, which is what they mean when they say things along the lines of "we are also in prison," or when pris-oners say, "For me, it's not so bad; it's hard for my family ..."

The sentiment that the criminal justice system is inhumane, viscerally felt by relatives and friends of incarcerated people, results, at least partially, from the random forms of control to which they are subjected and from the uneven application of regulations. Certain things are permitted in one institution and prohibited in another, even in France, where the implementation of European prison rules established in 2006 sought to standardize regulations.[26] Furthermore, many decisions have an arbitrary or discretionary aspect: how and when visitor permits are granted, whether or not permission to bring in clean laundry and books is given, or the degree to which there is surveillance during in-person visits. Additionally, the practical, social, and financial difficulties faced by relatives and friends are seldom taken into account. Visiting hours, for example, are often incompatible with regular employment hours, and prisons tend to be difficult to access by public transportation.

Visiting conditions, too, are often disgraceful and feel, to relatives and friends of incarcerated people, akin to an additional humiliation. They often say that they are treated "like dogs." Indeed, visiting rooms are generally dirty and sordid places in which the absence of privacy—including during visits when children are present—is often experienced as an unjustified punishment inflicted on innocent relatives and friends. The repression of intimacy,[27] which is certainly experienced differently according to the length of a sentence and the type of correctional institution in which the person is incarcerated,[28] and the disgraceful conditions in which the few sexual relationships that are allowed to take place, are perceived as infantilizing, humiliating, or traumatizing. Because of these conditions and the generally short visiting times, visiting rooms often feel like a "mere formality," stripping relational bonds of any depth.

"Wives of ..."

Many women lack the necessary resources to deal with a hardship that is, in fact, hardly exceptional.[29] The incarceration of a loved one, especially at the beginning of the sentence, and more so if they are a legal spouse, means taking on new responsibilities in the form of both personal and financial problems. Women are also often forced to take on more domestic work, now from a distance, and emotional labor—which is undervalued—for the benefit of the incarcerated person. In the language of French prisons, a woman supporting her incarcerated partner is said to "follow" him, which echoes what many women feel when they say that the incarceration of their partner has turned them into "prisoners' wives."

But the solidarity of relatives and friends is a resource for prisoners. Those with support, who have someone waiting for their release, stand in contrast to the "indigent." Post-release for the former is incomparable to that of the latter. For incarcerated men, and sometimes even for their fellow prisoners, women are a resource because of the many forms of support they can offer from the outside (besides domestic work). In correctional institutions where prisoners serve longer sentences, visits represent a true "distinction" between the two groups, just like regular correspondence. Indeed, less than a tenth of prisoners in these prisons receive regular visits. Overall, bonds with the outside create a sense of pride for the incarcerated, enabling them to face staff members as "a person (a man) like any other." This arises in part through this access to women, and thus to sexuality (and especially heterosexuality).

Although certain forms of control are exercised by incarcerated men over women, such as their availability, some women, paradoxically, gain autonomy when their partner is incarcerated, and thus are no longer "always on their backs."[30] Prison allows certain women, whether they are forced to work or travel alone for visits, to feel liberated—and sometimes to be literally liberated from harmful heterosexual relationships.

Resistance

Relatives and friends of incarcerated people do not climb the prison walls. They do not set fire to visiting rooms. Radical press outlets rarely publish anything written by them that might speak to the injustices that they endure, to their sufferings or their hopes. But they, too, resist. Being there, each week, at the prison gates. Sending money every month. Sending care packages when allowed. Lugging bags of laundry over and over. These forms of presence are resistance because prison is there to destroy the bonds that enable prisoners to be more than "inmates." With these bonds they remain friends, colleagues, fathers, sisters, etc. Their presence, and the discomfort they cause by exercising our rights, creates breaches in the prison walls.

Our forms of resistance deserve greater respect. Our status as relatives and friends of prisoners makes us vulnerable. Visitor passes always hang by a thread, and these passes are sometimes our most precious possessions. They link us to loved ones. They are our strength and our weakness, and the prison administration, as well as the guards, know this. And so it is particularly unjust that our resistance is often unseen and politically devalued by abolitionist movements, since our actions are dismissed for being motivated by our subjectivity, and/or for the legitimist views (see chapter 5) that many among us hold.

I know what it costs (not only from a material and financial point of view) to be "present." We've been told a thousand times that "he'll leave [you] when he gets out," and that if "he loved [you], he wouldn't be in prison." We have learned to ignore stares from passersby as we wait at the prison gates, and how to respond to harmful remarks from social workers and derogatory comments from guards. Our resistance is enduring all of that and still being here.

I have often heard men refuse to visit an incarcerated loved one under the pretext of their incapacity to control their reactions when faced with prison, and the contempt of the guards in particular. This is a way of communicating that we women who go to the visiting rooms and cherish our visitor passes are less radical than these men, and that agreeing to respect the rules there, where access is conditional, means accepting the existence of prison. But we accept it no more than the people who refuse to visit their incarcerated loved ones due to their sense of radicalism and of themselves. That, however, is a poor understanding of what the visiting room—and prison—is. Where else are the rules as systematically disputed, contested, and subverted?

There are many forms of resistance undertaken by relatives and friends. Some women throw themselves into judicial and/ or media battles on behalf of their husband or child (often a son), while others draft petitions denouncing the behavior of guards, or of a sentencing judge who does not grant enough early releases. There are also some women who dispute policies that allow guards to search their bags when entering prisons, or refuse to leave visiting rooms. But these forms of resistance are often invisible, because cases of collective resistance are rare and sporadic. They are also often denigrated because they fall short of an act of violence that might evoke images of the walls coming down.

Bring In or Let Out

Within the context of longer prison sentences and increasing numbers of prisoners, there is some fear that there is less concern for "letting out" prisoners than there is for "bringing in" relatives and friends to prison for longer and more private visits. This has caused abolitionist movements to struggle to integrate the issues surrounding the relatives and friends of prisoners into their work. Furthermore, there has been a weakening of the distinction between *inside* and *outside* for prisoners with increasing access to telephones—a development that is sometimes ambiguous for the spouses and partners of prisoners, since it has the potential to enable a form of control over the latter by the former. The fading distinction between *inside* and *outside* can be seen more overtly in the development of the ankle monitor, often presented as "progress" (being at home rather than in prison). But this progress is relative (since the home becomes a prison), especially considering the constraints that the devices put on relatives and friends, for whom the mental toll and logistical obligations linked to respecting the timeframes imposed by electronic monitoring can be greater than visits.

There has been increasing usage of video calls in the United States. In certain prisons, they are even replacing in-person visits, a fact that should be enough to dampen any enthusiasm there might be about access to this technology for prisoners and their relatives and friends. This increase primarily benefits the companies that offer these services, such as JPay (see insert on p. 85). Like the ankle monitor, there are also financial benefits for the correctional institutions and more broadly for the criminal justice system. These developments allow prisons to reduce movement within prisons and thus the number of prison employees, while also reducing the square footage of correctional institutions, because they require fewer cells and visiting rooms.

5

Penal Abolitionism and Feminism

The three previous chapters have shown that women should not expect anything from the criminal justice system, and that they are affected, in specific ways, by its existence. So what is to be made of the battles that have been waged in legal and judicial domains "in the name of women"? Are these battles the most efficient in terms of advancing feminism? Unlike the dominant strains of feminism, abolition feminism argues that legal and judicial battles do not represent the best approach for *all* women.

Carceral Feminism

The lack of interest among feminist movements in women impacted by prison is obvious. How often are incarcerated women discussed? How many times have feminist organizations protested in front of prisons for women? Who is organizing protests for incarcerated women? What material and political solidarities exist among women who have relatives and friends in prison?

Does the Women's Cause Stop at Courtroom Doors and Prison Gates?

Prison is a blind spot for contemporary feminist movements, with the notable exception of the unjust convictions of certain women who had been victims of violence, like the case of

Jacqueline Sauvage mentioned in chapter 2. For the most part, these movements care little for criminalized women or those who have relatives and friends in prison. But this has not always been the case.

The philanthropic movement that accompanied the first wave of feminism[1] in Western countries was greatly interested in prisons for women. In the United States, attention was focused on white women with whom the reformists—who were also white—identified.[2] This movement resulted in policies of incarcerating white women (who were considered to be in need of being "reformed") in separate units from men. African-American women, excluded from that sisterhood, remained in prisons for men.

So what explains this absence of interest in incarcerated women or those who have relatives and friends in prison? The answer to that question can be found within the feminist movements themselves, specifically in the ways that dominant movements privilege the perspective of certain women. These are women who, due to their class, race, or sexuality, are less susceptible to being criminalized themselves or having criminalized relatives and friends. Simone de Beauvoir famously pointed out the fragility of sisterhood (and of solidarity among women) as it pertains to class and race: "As bourgeois women, they are in solidarity with bourgeois men and not with women proletarians; as white women, they are in solidarity with white men and not with black women."[3] In other words, the answer to the question "Who is the political subject of feminism?" matters greatly, because it informs the way that the criminal justice system is viewed from a feminist perspective.

Carceral Feminism

Karlene Faith describes the "resistance to criminality" as a "feminist imperative."[4] Suffice to say that this is a minority perspective within feminism. Indeed, as many authors have pointed out, since its second wave—in other words, the 1970s—feminism has been characterized by a "growth of carceralism,"[5] to echo a phrase used by Elizabeth Bernstein,[6] who points to a "rise of carceral politics." Furthermore, as described by Roger Lancaster, the feminist agenda has taken an increasingly punitive turn, and criminal policies have given it greater space.[7] Two issues in particular have exacerbated these tendencies: sexual abuse and violence against women.

The invention of the phrase "carceral feminism" can be attributed to Elizabeth Bernstein, but it is now widely used in the anglophone world.[8] The phrase points out "a cultural and political formation in which previous generations' justice and liberation struggles are recast in carceral terms."[9] In other words, prison sentences have become central to contemporary demands made by feminist movements. This trend is manifested in the shift, beginning in the 1970s, toward the increased use of the judicial system in these struggles, notably from the perspective of the criminalization of discrimination.[10] As suggested by Kristin Bumiller, this punitive turn that feminism has taken is not unrelated to the ways in which the neoliberal state has appropriated feminist struggles against sexual violence.[11] And this tendency has been reinforced by movements against "modern slavery" and the "trafficking of women"—expressions whose questionable usage was discussed in chapter 1.[12]

As Jean Bérard[13] recounts, the French feminist movement of the 1970s was split on the issue of the criminalization of rape, in particular after the first convictions by the Courts of Assize. For example, there was Martine Storti, who wrote an opinion piece in *Libération* on February 24, 1978, titled "Rape: Twenty Years, It's Not Possible." By placing the focus on the sentence and by transforming it into a critique of the criminal justice system, a dissident voice was able to emerge. There was also Agnès Ouin, who wrote at about the same time: "Rape recognized as a crime by the criminal justice system, just like bank robbery or home burglary, what a victory! To battle for the recognition of rape as a crime, by an institution that has notions of crime that are completely whimsical and unique to it, which we are also combating, what derision!"[14]

The scope of violence against women and the dissatisfaction of victims (even when the sexual harm that they have suffered has been addressed by the criminal justice system) points to the failure of the judicial approach, which the majority of feminist movements have resorted to for several decades now. Using the law as a weapon does not appear to be the most efficient approach to confronting and defeating the patriarchy. Furthermore, the criminal justice system is a mechanism of the state, and it is therefore unrealistic to hope for any kind of emancipation from it. But it is still undeniably difficult to convey that punitive measures are not solutions. Beyond these abstract arguments, I will examine a more concrete issue: the effects of harsher criminal policies surrounding domestic violence in the United Sates.

Harsher Domestic Violence Criminal Policies in the United States

In the United States, the toughening of criminal policies against male perpetrators of domestic violence is the direct result of feminist struggles. And yet, it is also feminists who have formulated the most radical critiques of these very policies. Indeed, these policies have not led to a decrease in the number of female victims but to an increase in the number of poor, nonwhite, and/or immigrant men who have been incarcerated and/or deported.[15] Not only does criminal justice intervention in these matters fail to protect women (as a whole); it often brings them further harm. The African-American researcher and activist Beth Richie has shown that mandatory arrest policies that apply to every report of domestic violence (a demand made by many feminist organizations) have led to the arrest of more women and queer people, especially those who are racialized and poor, even when they were the same people who reported the violence.[16]

Police tend not to consider racialized and poor people as real victims, and might decide to arrest them rather than their attackers, or decide that the responsibility for the violence is shared, and thus arrest everyone involved. This generalized recourse to the criminal justice system in order to combat domestic violence has not decreased these incidents, and the primary effect has been a further criminalization not only of men, but also of women. Furthermore, although the number of women killed by their partner has not been reduced, the number of men killed by women in situations of self-defense has diminished. In other words: the measures taken have not protected women, but, by allowing some women to leave their home and thus avoid finding themselves in situations in which they might have resorted to homicide, these measures have led to a reduction in the number of male victims, as well as the number of women being criminally prosecuted for having defended themselves.[17] Taken as a whole, this is an outcome that appears, in the end, to benefit men more than women.

Calls for Increased Criminalization ... but of Whom?

Carceral feminism inspires the majority of legal proposals meant to address violence against women: the creation of new categories of crime (such as incest or femicide); the reduction, or the elimination, of the prescriptive period (for offenses of a sexual nature); harsher sentences; and various innovations that aim to systematize indictments and prosecutions.

Calls for the criminalization of "street harassment" fit perfectly into the expansion of carceral feminism. Its criminalization primarily impacts young men, who are racialized and/or working class, and whose predominance in public spaces is a result of their often limited access to private or social spaces.

Like Megan's Laws in the United States (see chapter 2), the position that the issue of street harassment (as well as cyber harassment) now occupies in feminist movements is shifting the focus to people outside of women's social circles, while in fact most acts of violence against women are perpetrated by someone they know.

The Instrumentalization of Women's Causes by "Penal Populism"

Never has war been waged against the patriarchy. However, women's oppression sometimes serves as justification for imperialist wars, as it did during the recent US war in Afghanistan. It is the same for criminal policies, a phenomenon known as "penal populism."[18] This term connotes the way criminal policies, by building on victims' movements and reactionary sentiments, have frequently used women to justify more and more repressive policies.

Criminal policies regarding sexual violence, domestic violence, or sex work (understood as "sex slavery") claim to "save" women by criminalizing certain men. Women's causes serve as pretexts for the expansion of the definitions of felonies and misdemeanors, the lengthening of sentences, but also for criminal innovations such as the ankle monitor, systematic DNA tests, etc. Does all of this really benefit women? Do these measures truly allow for a reduction in harm?

"Our Only Possibility"

The boundaries of carceral feminism[19] are imprecise, given, as Chloë Taylor remarks, that no one explicitly advocates in its name, even though it is the main source of inspiration for feminist movements that focus on male violence.[20] She points out that only the scholar Lise Gottell has tried to defend it, by arguing that laws and convictions might contribute to the amplification of victims' voices, and to changes surrounding the mentalities and norms concerning relationships between men and women.[21]

This reasoning, however, is precarious, because the gains (for certain women) are often surpassed by the undesirable side effects (for many other women and for certain men). But the primary weakness of carceral feminism is its tactical proposition. Although its claims are to be taken seriously (see above), and while its proposals (in France) would mean incarcerating hundreds of thousands of men for rape and sexual assault (see chapter 2 on the scope of victimhood), they would also mean imposing hundreds of thousands of fines for street harassment annually. How can all of this be considered a feminist victory? Not to mention that the deterrence effect of prison sentences (which is to say the impact fear of imprisonment has on the number of offenses committed) is very uncertain.

In response to this tactical impasse, penal abolitionism represents "our only possibility," a conclusion shared by Morgan Bassichis, Alexander Lee, and Dean Spade in light of their queer perspective on abolitionism.[22] If carceral feminism is promoted by certain women who have nothing to lose by furthering it, the most marginalized people view abolitionism not as a form of utopia, but as a way of avoiding the perpetual reproduction of systems of domination that the criminal justice system upholds (for example, by punishing poor and people of color even more).

Penal Abolitionism Is Feminist and Queer

Chapter 1 discussed the difficulty of defining penal abolitionism because of the diversity of its theoretical development and of the movements advocating for it. Below I will reestablish the profound connections that it maintains with feminism and LGBTQ movements. Although it is often understood that abolitionism is necessarily anticapitalist and that it fights against white supremacy, to present penal abolitionism as essentially feminist and queer is unfortunately rare.

Abolitionism Is Feminist

It is difficult to define abolition feminism because, as with abolitionism in general, there is such richness in its theoretical and strategic development. A certain number of women who have contributed to its growth can nevertheless be identified, beginning with Angela Davis (see insert on p. 24). Beth Richie, Julia C. Oparah, Ruth Wilson Gilmore, and Karlene Faith must also be cited. The contributions of women of color to the advances of abolition feminism are considerable[23]—and logical, given that the criminalization of people of color and the victimhood of women of color are standard entry points for abolition feminism analyses. These arguments have been further shaped by reflections on women incarcerated for domestic violence, as well as sexual violence in prisons for women (as is the case with Joan Little, see insert on p. 69).[24]

Abolition feminism does not define itself as either a current within the larger feminist movement or as a strain of penal abolitionism, but rather as a collaboration between feminism and penal abolitionism. Indeed, early penal abolitionism recognized what it owed to feminism:[25] feminism gave penal abolitionism the tools necessary to critique the criminal justice system, to the extent that a co-construction of abolitionism by feminism can be imagined. As Brian D. MacLean and Hal Pepinsky note, "feminist thinking not only informs our abolitionist stance, but is central to it."[26]

The role played by feminism in abolitionism is explained by its focus on certain central themes and their respective places within the law: domestic work (to which labor law does not apply), and sexual harm and violence (which criminal and civil law do address). On the issues of abortion and sexual harm, feminism, by demanding the decriminalization of one and the criminalization of the other, has also shown that any critique of the criminal justice system must take power relations based on gender into account, and that any analytical framework established solely in terms of social classes—which only denounces "bourgeois" justice—is not enough.

Penal Abolitionism Is Queer

In the United States, abolitionist movements have been criticized for their tendency to fail to take queer people into account, especially queer people of color.[27] Little place is made for LGBTQ people and issues in abolitionist struggles—beyond the sole question of the inclusion or visibility of LGBTQ people (see chapter 6). However, the existence of the criminal justice system affects them proportionally more than the rest of the population, because of the forms of victimhood and prosecution that are specific to the criminalization of queerness (see chapters 2 and 3). Nevertheless, in recent years, abolitionist movements in the United States have tried to remedy this blind spot, spurred simultaneously by the increasingly prominent positions of queer groups (see below) and by the publication of more and more queer research on the criminal justice system. To cite just one example among many, Eric A. Stanley and Nat Smith coedited a book entitled *Captive Genders*,[28] published in 2011 and republished in 2015 with an introduction by CeCe McDonald (see insert on p. 48).

Penal abolitionism is strongly tied to the history of the LGBTQ liberation movement.[29] First because queer communities have acquired invaluable experience managing problematic situations outside of the criminal justice system, and this experience has been a source of inspiration for the entirety of the abolitionist movement. Additionally, as a result of the LGBTQ community's long history of criminalization, LGBTQ movements have produced radical critiques of police, of prisons, and of the legal system. Take, for example, the LGBTQ pride parades that happen around the world each year in June, which commemorate the Stonewall riots in New York City in June 1969 and that were a response to police violence against queer people.

That political lineage is still present in the denunciation, by some LGBTQ movements, of pinkwashing,[30] a term for when police and prisons participate in LGBTQ pride marches, or establishing programs specifically for LGBTQ people (specific procedures for LGBTQ victims, protection of incarcerated LGBTQ people, etc.). Some LGBTQ organizations also take clear stances against "queer punitivity"[31]—an expression related to the call, by some LGBTQ movements, for increased use of the criminal justice system to keep queer people safe from violence (just as "carceral feminism" designates this type of position within feminism).

Movements against queer punitivity are growing in North America, as shown by the exclusion, in 2017, of uniformed police officers from the LGBTQ pride parade in Toronto. In the United States, numerous queer collectives are involved in penal abolitionism, such as Black and Pink (see insert on p. 75); Project Nia; the Transgender, Gender Variant, and Intersex (TGI) Justice Project; Queers for Economic Justice (New York); and the collective Against Equality,[32] which does the important work of disseminating queer and abolitionist research, notably the work of Ryan Conrad.[33] Furthermore, the Trans Prisoner Day of Action and Solidarity, which has taken place every January 22 since 2015, started by Marius Mason, is a rallying point between abolitionist and queer movements. In France, queer critiques of the criminal justice system or of the police remain rare, even if the presence of Flag! floats (an association of LGTBQ police and gendarmes) in LGBTQ pride parades is more and more controversial and the slogan "Pas de police dans mes fiertés!" (No cops at Pride!) is increasingly popular.

Among others, Morgan Bassichis, Alexander Lee, and Dean Spade call on LGBTQ movements to "reclaim a radical legacy,"[34] as expressed, for example, in the speeches of Sylvia Rivera in 1973 (see insert on p. 104). But as emphasized by Vanessa R. Panfil, criminalized queer people have been rendered invisible within LGBTQ movements (except in cases of the criminalization of homosexuality), and this is not a mistake: it stems from strategic choices made by the dominant currents within LGBTQ movements, made up primarily of white and middle- or upper-class people.[35] But political invisibility is not incompatible with eroticization and fetishization: thus the prevalence, in France, of "racaille" (scum) and "beur" (an offensive term used to refer to French-born people whose parents are North African immigrants) figures in gay porn. Needless to say, this characterization is not a form of political solidarity with those who are statistically at the greatest risk of sexual violence in French prisons. In the same vein, there are legitimate questions surrounding the sexual fetishization, in some LGBTQ pornography, of prison and law enforcement professions (for example, uniforms and props). Queer organizations' protests against the "WE Party Prison of Love," a party organized in San Francisco in June 2014 during the weekend of that city's LGBTQ pride parade, pointed out the incongruity of such a party, especially given the scope of the criminalization of LGBTQ people—but this is a position that is, unfortunately, still too rare.

Abolitionist Movements and the Cause of Women

What place is there for women in abolitionist movements? What forms of exclusion do they endure? What constraints do they encounter in these movements? Are they really considered the political subjects of abolitionist fights?

"Y'all better quiet down"

Sylvia Rivera, who was Latin American, was a member of the small group of people who founded the Gay Liberation Front (GLF) in New York after the 1969 Stonewall riots, in which she participated alongside many other trans women of color. The following year, along with her friend Marsha P. Johnson, she created the organization Street Transvestite Action Revolutionaries (STAR), who gathered and welcomed young drag queens and trans women of color. Sylvia Rivera fought all her life for poor and non-white queer people. She died in 2002.

In honor of this emblematic figure of gay, queer, and trans liberation movements in the United States, the Sylvia Rivera Law Project was created. This organization, based in New York City, provides legal aid to trans, intersex, and gender nonconforming people, and maintains correspondence with them in prison. It also wages political campaigns for the rights of incarcerated trans people.

On June 24, 1973, during a gay pride parade in New York City, Sylvia Rivera attacked the mainstream gay movement in a speech that remains celebrated.[36] Her way of speaking reflects the absence, at the time, of the use of the term "trans," and the ways in which the term "gay" might obscure it:

> Y'all better quiet down. I've been trying to get up here all day for your gay brothers and your gay sisters in jail, that write me every motherfucking week and ask for your help, and you all don't do a goddamn thing for them.
>
> Have you ever been beaten up and raped and jailed? Now think about it. They've been beaten up and raped after they've had to spend much of their money in jail to get their [inaudible], and try to get their sex changes. The women have tried to fight for their sex changes or to become women. On the women's liberation and they write STAR, not to the women's groups, they do not write women, they do not write men, they write STAR because we're trying to do something for them.

> *I have been to jail. I have been raped. And beaten. Many times! By men, heterosexual men that do not belong in the homosexual shelter. But, do you do anything for me? No. You tell me to go and hide my tail between my legs. I will not put up with this shit. I have been beaten. I have had my nose broken. I have been thrown in jail. I have lost my job. I have lost my apartment for gay liberation and you all treat me this way? What the fuck's wrong with you all? Think about that!*
>
> *I do not believe in a revolution, but you all do. I believe in the gay power. I believe in us getting our rights, or else I would not be out there fighting for our rights. That's all I wanted to say to you people. If you all want to know about the people in jail and do not forget Bambi L'Amour, and Dora Mark, Kenny Metzner, and other gay people in jail, come and see the people at Star House.*
>
> *The people are trying to do something for all of us, and not men and women that belong to a white, middle-class white club. And that's what you all belong to!*
> *REVOLUTION NOW! GAY POWER!*

Women and Feminism in Abolitionist Struggles

In abolitionist (especially anti-prison) struggles, there are often fewer women than men, and women's experiences are not always positive, because of the sexism that can (as elsewhere) exist in these spaces. Furthermore, women involved in these struggles, especially those who have been victims of sexual harm or of violence, might harbor ambiguous sentiments. They might believe in the political aspirations of the struggle without recognizing the type of victimhood they have themselves endured or the absence of concrete solutions that have been offered to them. It is sometimes worse. Attackers sometimes take advantage of the ways in which, in certain movements, critique of the criminal justice system is accompanied by a lack of accountability for instances of harm. And so certain men, to evade responsibilities, exploit the critiques of punitive approaches developed by abolitionism (see chapter 6).

Nearly three decades ago, Martin Schwartz and Walter DeKeseredy observed the rarity of accommodations made for rape victims within abolitionist movements.[37] This unfortunately remains rather true: abolitionist movements, specifically in France, do not focus on sexual violence very often. Indeed, their analyses tend to put off addressing this problem (how exactly is unclear) until the Revolution (see chapter 6).

In a joint statement made in 2001, Incite! and Critical Resistance pointed out the lack of concern for violence against women as one of the main weaknesses of abolitionist movements. The two organizations indicated that "until these strategies [for addressing the rampant forms of violence women face] are developed, many women will feel shortchanged by the movement."[38] Furthermore, as pointed out by the Canadian Adina Ilea, the "dangerous few" argument, copiously used in abolitionist movements, ignores the question of sexual victimhood, despite its sometimes significant and lasting impacts.[39]

Abolitionist movements often cultivate a justified sensitivity to class- and race-based oppressions, as well as to the ways in which they are concretely experienced by criminalized populations. Other forms of oppression, in particular those linked to gender and sexuality, generally draw less attention. This oversight is all the more troubling since the devastating overall effect of prison—its social costs—is certainly the most powerful argument that could be made in denouncing its existence and supporting its abolition. Even when incarcerated women are referenced in conversations about prisoners, the specific forms of their criminalization and the sentences they serve are rarely emphasized.

Victoria Law, among others, has noted just how little interest there is surrounding issues pertaining to incarcerated women and prisons for women (such as sexual harm committed in prison, or the difficulty of obtaining menstrual hygiene products and accessing certain care).[40] She also notes that inmate revolts in prisons for women elicit far less attention and support than those in prisons for men. It is often said that nothing happens in prisons for women. Protests there can take a variety of forms, but they are rendered invisible because they do not involve violence, which is the standard form of protest within abolitionist movements.

Who Is the Political Subject of Abolitionist Fights?

In abolitionist movements, two figures elicit instant sympathy: the escapee and the rioter. Whether or not they succeed in their escape, whether they stand on a prison's roof or end up in a disciplinary cell, the escapee and the rioter are generally considered unassailable figures in the anticarceral struggle. More generally, any man in prison will elicit more sympathy from the simple fact of being in prison than the woman who provides them with material, financial, and emotional support—and who sometimes, if her husband, partner, brother, or son has escaped or rebelled, was herself an accomplice to the escape or communicated his demands and organized his defense. The woman, preoccupied by the material and financial survival of her household, who might bitterly resent the prisoner for his incarceration and who might feel that he deserves his punishment, or express some form of relief, is rarely welcome in anticarceral movements.

Resolutely evoking the role of women, victims, or relatives and friends of prisoners within abolitionist struggles seems productive to me. It might prove useful in moving beyond the "carceral-centric"[41] critique that frequently reduces these struggles to just what happens inside the prison walls. They are often more concerned with what happens inside prisons than with the ways in which prisons are part of a larger system intended to discipline those on the *inside* at least as much as those on the *outside,* and a narrow focus on the prison itself overlooks those who assume a significant portion of the social costs of prison. By focusing much more on the fate of prisoners rather than on the harm that prison does to society (notably for the victims), these struggles promote a moral debate (against the disgraceful condition imposed on some) that hinders the political goal: a society without prison.

In addition, approaching abolitionist struggles from a feminist perspective can show how women are rendered invisible in many abolitionist struggles, but can also show how their own battles and forms of resistance, *inside* and *outside*, remain unseen. This approach calls the insurrectionist[42] primacy of certain abolitionist movements into question, at least on the European continent, and questions the place of violence in the collective action toolkit—not because women resort to violence less often, or because insurrectionist strategies should be disqualified, but because diverse strategies should be employed within abolitionist movements, and because abolitionism cannot be built solely on supporting prison riots.

The Sexual Division of Activist Work

Within abolitionist movements, women are confronted with the same difficulties that arise in other activist spaces, such as less active roles in decision-making processes and more limited opportunities to speak. These difficulties go hand in hand with other forms of division, between men and women, of tasks linked to political, material, and emotional solidarity. Without lingering on the most stereotypical scenarios (for example, a woman reading a communiqué written by a man to the press, or at a protest), it should be noted that women already take on (or are assigned) the tasks of transporting laundry to arrested comrades, of sending money orders (even if the money is being given by men), and of keeping in touch with lawyers. More than anything they are responsible for maintaining correspondence and making visits and, in these ways, providing moral support. As a woman (but also as a person with loved ones who were in prison), I have experienced, endured, and observed this sexual division within activist work and have noted how, involuntarily, I became the one with the skills necessary to take care of people (generally men) who had been arrested or incarcerated. But it is much more difficult to discuss this particular issue since the need for these skills generally arises in moments of crisis, and a broad resolution to change collective and individual practices requires long-term involvement and planning.

Women with incarcerated relatives and friends face an additional difficulty: they are often assigned the role of witness or messenger to the outside world, and from this role gain a measure of respect within the movement. However, they are listened to for what they have witnessed and for the messages (from men) that they communicate, not for what they experience, think, and must process themselves. This observation is part of the general critique of the roles often assigned to those who are incarcerated, or who have been previously incarcerated.[43] Furthermore, the ways in which relatives and friends (like prisoners) are treated in certain movements sometimes stems from fetishization or tokenism.[44] To be blunt, there's a tendency to view relatives and friends of prisoners (much like prisoners or victims of state crimes) as inherently infallible, and to focus political activity solely in support of their struggles. Previously incarcerated people are often called on to testify to their "lived experience" and share their "perspective." In both cases, these tendencies arise from a refusal to consider these people as full political subjects, people who fight alongside us, people who can be wrong or with whom disagreements might arise.

The sexual division of activist work observed in abolitionist struggles is not specific to these movements. There is a striking resemblance to the division that exists within the struggles against state crimes (whose victims are mainly men). In both cases, women fight for men. But the "visibility" of women (the token woman as the muse) does not protect them from the typical reification of the patriarchal order. Can women exist politically without being the "wife of" or the "mother of"? Are women not affected by the existence of the criminal justice system, prison, and the police—and not only as the "wife of" or the "mother of"? What do women have to say about it?

Why Are There So Few of Us?

When considering the topic of women in abolitionist movements, relatives and friends of prisoners are of particular concern to me. I have reflected on their place in abolitionist struggles and formulated a few propositions (see insert on p. 111).[45] These reflections are borne from my surprise, during my early involvement in abolitionism, at meeting so few other relatives and friends—and at realizing that we are so rarely noticed. In light of my experience—in the visiting rooms and in anticarceral fights—I have a few hypotheses about why this is the case. First of all, a woman's personal encounter with prison might lead, naturally, to a refusal to give it any more mental space—especially if participating in an abolitionist movement implies dismal meetings and activities where one might risk dealing with activists who, while sincere, are sometimes far more versed in theoretical notions about prison than in its concrete realities.[46]

Nevertheless, abolitionist movements bear full responsibility for how few relatives and friends of prisoners populate their ranks, because they rarely provide themselves the opportunity to meet these people. All they would have to do is go to the prison gates. It is certainly thankless activist work, but no more so than distributing leaflets outside of the subway. Abolitionist movements must confront some of their biases and modes of operation.

> **"Manifesto for Prisoners' Relatives and Friends"**
>
> 1. There is no abolitionist movement without prisoners' relatives and loved ones.
> 2. The specific ways in which women are affected by the existence of prisons must be analyzed and taken into consideration in the struggle for penal abolition.
> 3. The relatives and loved ones of prisoners are neither mere witnesses nor allies of abolitionist struggles; they are the political subjects of these struggles.
> 4. Abolitionist struggles must promote the empowerment of prisoners' relatives and loved ones and promote the development of political, material, and emotional solidarity among them.
> 5. Abolitionist struggles must avoid paternalistic assistance to prisoners' relatives and loved ones and lead the fight against the nonprofit-industrial complex.

Prison Legitimism among Relatives and Friends of Prisoners

Many relatives and friends of prisoners are legitimists: they believe the carceral system to be a legitimate one that serves a legitimate purpose. Many prisoners are as well, but this has never led to their position within the abolitionist movement being called into question. To tell the truth, the legitimism that prisoners and their relatives and friends espouse is a normal result of their experiences with injustice, which is more often processed as an individual fate than as a collective condition that can be questioned.

In addition to this legitimism, relatives and friends (especially women) are sometimes reproached for submission to the criminal justice system.[47] Abolitionist movements are easily seduced by the specter of the prisoner who is completely defiant of prison order. If women are less enthusiastic in this regard, it is perhaps because they have other responsibilities (especially if they take care of children). I remember the night when I realized this: the day before a visit, I was in lodging for visitors of prisoners and had struck up a conversation with a woman whose companion had attempted to escape. She described herself as being distinctly relieved that he had failed. She was angry with him: she hoped that the father of her children would finally take on some of the responsibility that she had been bearing, on her own, for many years. She was thus even more hopeful that he would do whatever was necessary to obtain an early release, rather than opting for an escape attempt, which, if it had succeeded, would have actually prevented him from being present for his children in an enduring way.

Many prisoners' relatives and friends do not take the idea of prison abolition seriously. Certain mothers are relieved that their sons were incarcerated rather than killed during a robbery, or dead of an overdose. Certain women hope that after incarceration, their spouse will better fulfill his conjugal and parental roles. All of these lines of thinking reflect the notion that in the world as it is, prison is the lesser of two evils. I consider relatives' and friends' legitimism a contradiction that needs to be addressed, but also as an entry point for abolitionist struggles, since this population is not, on the whole, abolitionist.

Social Distance and Female Solidarity

From the perspective of race and class, abolitionist activists are often very distinct from prisoners and those who have relatives and friends in prison. Jodie M. Lawston has observed this characteristic in the United States, but this can be seen in France as well, where these differences sometimes render the formation of a real sisterhood between *inside* and *outside* difficult.[48] The social gap between the two groups is aggravated by the tendency of abolitionist movements to situate themselves within an activist subculture, with its interconnectivity and unique inner workings.[49] This subculture is accompanied by general activist know-how and communication skills (writing political texts, public speaking, respecting procedural rules, etc.) whose discussion,[50] sharing, and transmission is rarely formalized.

Women who have relatives and friends in prison and are involved in abolitionist movements are rarely very representative of the women in visiting rooms. They are often among the most equipped socially and economically, and their relatives and friends in prison might benefit from a certain prestige in prison. Thus we are often an "exception," as with the "politicized prisoners," and saying so is a way of emphasizing that we do not really belong among our peers.

I am often hurt to see how the families of incarcerated people are thought of as a homogeneous group with one shared viewpoint within abolitionist movements. Although attending to the unique nature of each situation makes it difficult to organize toward major political change, there must nevertheless be space for the variety of experiences of relatives and friends of prisoners. In a patriarchal society, saying that some women are involved due to love or familial obligation obviously fails to exhaust the complexity of reasons for why women can be in solidarity with relatives and friends in prison. It is thus important not to perpetuate the demand for conjugal and familial solidarity that is often imposed on women, and to make sure to concretely build feminist solidarities that contribute to the empowerment of women.

6

Emancipating Ourselves from the Criminal Justice System and Constructing Autonomy

The critical framework provided by abolitionism (chapter 1) allows for a methodical analysis of the effects of the existence of the criminal justice system on women (chapters 2, 3, and 4). This analysis shows the necessity of articulating the theoretical perspectives of abolitionism and feminism (chapter 5). But what political strategies should be adopted? This chapter explores the paths of reflection, the practices, and the experiences of people and groups who, especially through transformative justice, seek ways to free themselves from penal justice. All this must be read while keeping the modesty of penal abolitionism in mind: it invites creativity more than it offers ready-made solutions.

Strategies for Feminist and Queer Abolitionism

As shown by the critique of carceral feminism (chapter 5), using the law as a tool is never without complications. The idea of postponing the abolition of the criminal justice system until the Revolution must also be addressed. Women have waited long enough. Their position is unsatisfying from a pragmatic point of view: although one can hope for changes in relations of production and a more harmonious social life, it is difficult to imagine a world free from all forms of deviance.[1] The sociologist Émile Durkheim uses a rather revealing metaphor: "Imagine a community of saints in an exemplary and perfect monastery. In it, crime as such will be unknown, but faults that appear venial to the ordinary person will arouse the same sense of scandal that normal crimes do in ordinary consciences."[2] Since deviance will not disappear if there is a Revolution one day, there is no reason to postpone determining how to improve the ways that problematic situations are handled.

But do feminist and queer abolitionism have different strategic propositions than those of other abolitionist currents? Let's closely examine two proposals—the decarceralization of women, and the non-punitive handling of perpetrators of violence against women—that feminists have developed.

Decarceralization: Strategy or Tactic?

Certain feminists have proposed the decarceralization of women based on their lack of dangerousness[3] and/or the recognition of their specific needs.[4] This approach could include the decriminalization of drugs and activities linked to sex work. In addition to the impasses caused by gender-specific approaches explored in chapter 3, there are also limits to reductionist strategies (see chapter 1). Abolitionist thought has underlined the fact that the rhetoric of "the dangerous few" and innocentism does not undermine the arguments justifying the incarceration of certain people. More generally, these approaches ignore the factors that contribute to the criminalization of women, such as domestic violence, sexual abuse, or LGBTQ-phobia. Morgan Bassichis, Alexander Lee, and Dean Spade raise, from a queer abolitionist point of view, similar arguments to incorporate transformative justice into their struggles, a perspective that focuses on the structural reasons for the imprisonment of queer people. They take this approach instead of arguing in favor of queer decarceralization, which would risk distinguishing "deserving" victims from "undeserving" victims.[5]

On the other hand, the decarceralization of women might be a good tactical option, as proposed by the British criminologist Pat Carlen. Pat Carlen maintains that "it would be easier, initially, to convince the population to try to abolish prisons for women than prisons for men."[6] The decarceralization of women is conceivable—in the abolitionist fight, as a tactical demand, or a "card to play"—more so than the decarceralization of LGBTQ people. Such a tactic nevertheless risks falling into essentialist arguments about the "fragility" of women and the "unique" nature of their bonds with their children, not to mention essentialist ideas that women are less inherently violent than men.

Non-Punitive Treatment for Perpetrators

Certain feminists have called for the non-punitive treatment of perpetrators of violence against women. One of the first to emerge, in the 1980s, was Fay Honey Knopp, a Quaker, feminist, and abolitionist from the United States, who made this argument at a time when abolitionism was still content with the argument of the dangerous few (see chapter 1).[7] Knopp was convinced, like other activists working with perpetrators of sexual offenses, that the "least restrictive" and "most humane" responses were more effective than punitive approaches. She proposed an "attrition model," where "at the first sign of sexual aggression," perpetrators would be placed in reeducation facilities and integrated into a feminist environment.[8] As progressive as this sounds, there is reason to wonder if, given its mandatory nature, reeducation is really any different from punishment.

The limits of punitive approaches for sexual harm (see chapter 2) have inspired programs such as support and accountability circles, first developed in Canada in the mid-1990s,[9] and soon thereafter in the United Kingdom and in some US states. These programs rely on the "radical hospitality" and "intentional friendship" of volunteers, who form a "circle of care" around the person released from prison and help them to "find their place in the community."[10] Scientific evaluations of these methods are fiercely debated. Ian A. Elliott and Gary Zajac[11] assert that their efficiency is not at all proven, and question the number put forth by the first Canadian study of the risk of recidivism, which claimed to have reduced it by more than 83 percent when compared to other methods.[12]

Against Conspicuous Recourse to the Criminal Justice System

Chapter 2 explored certain issues that arise for victims when there is recourse to the criminal justice system, most notably the risk of "dependency" on criminal courts. I hope to return to this question from a more pragmatic point of view. Must the police be called? Must charges be brought? I am often asked these questions by people torn between their critiques of the criminal justice system and their needs as victims.

Recourse to Criminal Justice as Privilege

In general, recourse to criminal justice for violence against women is not often challenged. Some organizations that work with victims are careful not to involve themselves in the victim's decision to initiate legal proceedings or not, but the majority encourage them to do so. Even on the far left, where radical critiques of the state are more pronounced, recourse to criminal justice or to state institutions (for example, a police department's internal affairs bureau) is rarely the object of debate in cases of police or fascist violence. African-American poet and feminist Audre Lorde is often quoted in these circles: "The master's tools will never dismantle the master's house." But it is curiously not applied to the subject of the judicial system.

The capacity, or not, to rely on the criminal justice system is, however, tied to certain privileges, starting with citizenship or residency status. These privileges are based on personal characteristics and social skills that allow victims to conform to the roles expected of them (see chapter 2). Thus, certain people might choose not to file a complaint, because they are foreigners and undocumented, have no residency permit, and, consequently, fear being deported. Others might not because they themselves, or their relatives and friends, run the risk of being re-victimized by the police. The criminal justice system falls far short of offering solutions that everyone can rely on—not to mention that it does nothing to change the social conditions that rendered the harm possible in the first place.

A Matter of Principle?

I do not wish to turn the non-use of the criminal justice system into a matter of principle. I never critique people for whom it can fulfill certain needs. This has been the case for me, even though I already had a fairly clear idea of its problems. For many reasons that were not mine alone, I did not, at the time, have access to resources that in other circumstances might have allowed me to do without the criminal justice system. Beyond my particular background, I would like to insist that calling the police might often be the only solution in an emergency, when the physical or mental well-being of a person is threatened. In fact, non-use of the criminal justice system could also be tied to other types of privileges, beyond those previously evoked, such as the privilege of a protective family or community environment, support from relatives and friends, etc. Access to these resources being unequal, no one can be blamed for having turned to the criminal justice system in a particular circumstance. It seems necessary to me to insist on this point, because I have often heard, in "radical" milieus, criticism of women who have suffered violence at the hands of men and who have sought recourse in the criminal justice system, more so than in cases of male victims of fascist or state crimes.

All recourse to the criminal system is, in my view, a *collective failure* which must be grasped in order to reflect on *collective solutions*. Certain transformative justice groups (see below) have participants make diagrams during workshops in which they identify, in concentric circles, the people on whom they know they can rely. They share and discuss the resources they have access to (for when their physical or mental well-being is threatened), those that can be mobilized, and those that they lack; but also how to construct new resources, collectively.

Certain groups choose to exclude perpetrators from their spaces and sometimes make public the reason for the exclusion. This choice is unsatisfying, since it leaves the person excluded unchanged, along with the conditions that made their actions possible in the first place. When feminists make this kind of decision and target men, they are sometimes critiqued, often by other men, in the name of abolitionist principles and the "rejection of punishment." Beyond the oft-used dubious metaphor wherein abolitionist men compare being banned from a socializing space with imprisonment, these men's critiques are taken at face value as critiques made "on principle."[13] By not engaging themselves in a process of transformation (which would include the perpetrator and themselves), by leaving the task of securing their own safety to others, the people who issue these critiques do not contribute to the advancement of non-punitive practices in any way. In fact, they forget that they are just as responsible as the people who make this type of decision. (See below regarding transformative justice.)

Relying on Our Own Strength

There is no doubt that the criminal justice system itself must be combated more than the habit of using it. It is thus necessary to construct collective autonomy in order to manage difficult situations, and the first step is to take stock of our abundant skills in this regard. On an individual level, conflicts are resolved without calling on the criminal justice system every day: by mitigating a friend or relative's anger, by asking a third party to intervene in a dispute, by buying a drink for someone we have offended, etc. Because we so often use these approaches, we are rarely aware of these skills. On a collective level, we possess millennia of conflict resolution experience outside of the criminal justice system. The point here is not to romanticize past societies or distant cultures for not relying on prison-like systems, but to highlight the fact that the criminal justice system is not an insurmountable barrier, and that forms of restorative and transformative justice (explored below) have a long history, as evidenced by the precedents they have in Indigenous cultures of North America and Oceania (see insert on p. 128).

From Restorative Justice to Transformative Justice

Techniques for addressing harm outside of the criminal justice system emerged in the 1970s. They are the result of experiences that women acquired when building self-defense organizations and fostering community approaches to violence and sexual harm, largely within the women's movement and other liberationist movements.[14] Support groups for victims of sexual harm, who understood the exact limitations of the criminal justice from their own experience, also made significant contributions to these techniques.

Chapter 1 highlighted the fact that there are similar questions surrounding penal abolition and political and international conflict resolution. The latter types of conflict are not the subject of this book. It is, however, difficult to completely ignore them, especially given the ways in which, in recent decades, penal abolitionism has been fueled by criticism of international criminal justice[15] (such as tribunals),[16] but also by innovations in political transition[17] and transitional justice, such as Truth and Reparations Committees. The Truth and Reconciliation Commission of Canada, for example, implemented certain historic reparations for colonization.[18]

The techniques for addressing harm outside of the criminal justice system have been given various names: "reparative justice," "restorative justice," and "transformative justice." These three names cover closely related approaches and are sometimes thought to be different variants of the same idea.[19] All three refuse criminal justice confrontations between victim and perpetrator, instead opting for mediation, reconciliation, and healing (as much for the victim as for the community). The format of this book does not allow for an exhaustive discussion, but I will present a few of the main directives and go over a few reflections that can be drawn from this approach.

From Reparative Justice to Restorative Justice

Penal abolitionism has fostered the development of reparative justice, a technique that stems from critiques of the retributive nature of the criminal justice system. Reparative justice embraces the idea of "reintegrative shaming," as posited by the Australian John Braithwaite,[20] who drew inspiration from the way that in certain cultures, the condemnation of violence is not accompanied by the social exclusion of its perpetrator— the inverse of the Western criminal justice system. The ways parents can simultaneously express their disapproval for bad behavior but their love for their children is a familiar example of this kind of approach.

Feminists have called the effectiveness of reparative justice into question, especially in the context of gender violence.[21] The approach is particularly poorly equipped to guarantee the security of victims of domestic violence, given the dynamics specific to this kind of violence. C. Quince Hopkins and Mary

P. Koss assert that reparative justice, when dealing with sexual harm, works much better when the harm has been committed by a stranger rather than someone known to the victim.[22]

Restorative justice was born in the mid-1970s in North America. Closely related to the peacemaking of Hal Pepinsky and Richard Quinney,[23] it owes a great deal to Howard Zehr,[24] an American criminologist and member of the Mennonite church.[25] While its first iteration, reparative justice, entails monetary reparations and other forms of compensation, restorative justice insists on the "restoration" of social bonds and the resolution of a conflict or problem.[26] This approach translates to innovations, sometimes within the criminal justice system itself, such as meetings between the perpetrators and the victims (reconciliation circles) or family conferences (where relatives of minors participate to assist them in redressing whatever wrong they have caused).

Transformative Justice

The practices of transformative justice (TJ) were developed in the early 2000s, based on the concept of "community accountability"[27] first formulated by the activist group Incite! According to this concept, community accountability involves four components:

1) support for the victim, their safety, and their self-determination
2) accountability of the perpetrator and their change in behavior
3) community changes in favor of non-oppressive and non-violent values and practices
4) political and structural changes of the conditions that allow for the harm to take place.

The people who inspired TJ consistently evoke its creative dimension, and those who practice it often note its "DIY" nature. One of its principal founders, Ruth Morris (see insert on p. 126), wrote, "Transformative justice uses the power unleashed by the harm of a crime to let those most affected find truly creative, healing solutions."[28] TJ insists on the creative power of the survivors. It was greatly inspired by the means women of color (as shown by Black feminism) and LGBTQ people use to survive, despite their structural exclusion from the support provided to other victims—an exclusion that explains the crucial role that these communities play in the formation of TJ groups.

TJ was developed partly in reaction to the increased use of restorative justice by criminal justice systems. Canada has several hundred restorative justice programs.[29] TJ and the approaches that exist entirely outside of the criminal justice system are still in their infancy there.[30] The majority of active TJ services have been established by organizations in the United States. Among the most widely known is Creative Interventions (CI), founded in 2004 in Oakland, California, by Mimi Kim.[31] CI, which proposes community approaches to interpersonal violence, developed the Story Telling & Organizing Project (STOP), which is focused on domestic and family violence as well as on sexual harm, and offers resources for the establishment of community accountability practices.

In the United States, notable organizations include the Safe OUTside the System (SOS) Collective in New York, a group "by and for Lesbian, Gay, Bisexual, Two-Spirit,[32] Trans, and Gender Non Conforming people of color;" generationFIVE, whose goal is to end the sexual abuse of children within five generations; the Bay Area Transformative Justice Collective (BATJC) in the San Francisco area; and Communities Against Rape and Abuse (CARA) in Seattle. Few organizations of this kind exist in Europe, but there is the Community Accountability + Transformative Justice Collective Berlin, active in the German capital since 2011.

Beyond the practical knowledge that these groups have developed, they offer numerous manuals and protocols, of which the most renowned are those from CI[33] and *Toward Transformative Justice* by generationFIVE.[34]

Despite their variety, these approaches share at least four characteristics:

A collective process
This aspect groups together the victims, the perpetrators, and the community (the definition of "community" varies depending on the people involved in the process). TJ recognizes that responsibility for the harm cannot be attributed exclusively to the person who caused it. For this reason, and based on guidance from Louk Hulsman (see chapter 1), the expression "problematic situation" is generally preferred to "problematic behavior" or "problematic person."[35] The goal is to *resolve* a situation and not only *repair* a harm.

Individualization of the victim's need for security
TJ encourages victims to express their needs, which are inherently unique and can evolve over time.

TJ takes all power relations and their structural nature into consideration
This differs from the criminal justice system, which takes only the "context" of the act itself into account. Perpetrators and victims are involved in power relations that are often complex, and often linked to class, gender, and race. While criminal justice judges an *act*, TJ responds to the needs of *people*. For example, in the case of a homeless person of color who steals property, criminal justice sees a theft, while TJ takes the harm into consideration as well as the vulnerability of that person, and the structural difficulties they face.

Long-term Engagement
TJ takes a long time because it does not delegate the resolution of "problematic situations" to the criminal justice system, and because it is rarely a linear process.

"Even for Rape?"

Certain TJ organizations are primarily concerned with sexual harm, such as the Chrysalis Collective[36] and CARA. Among the most accessible resources here is *The Revolution Starts at Home*, which began as a zine written by activists and survivors of abuse that was distributed in the United States beginning in 2008 and published in book form in 2011.[37]

I will not detail the way these organizations work here, but I will respond to a few objections, beginning with a question often posed to abolitionists: "You're opposed to the criminal justice system ... even for rape?" There is substantial evidence that TJ, in light of the failure of criminal punishments for sexual harm,[38] offers solutions to survivors and allows for communities to reinforce vigilance, while establishing emancipation from the penal system and building autonomy.

The participation of both perpetrators and victims in TJ proceedings is sometimes misunderstood. It does not imply that men's violence is coproduced by perpetrators and victims

---

Ruth Morris (1933–2001)

Born in the United States in 1933, Ruth Morris was an activist against the Vietnam War, poverty, and racism. She emigrated to Canada in 1968 and there dedicated her activism to the criminal justice system. Ruth Morris developed the concept of "transformative justice," inspired partly by the justice practices of Indigenous people in Canada (see insert on p. 128) and in New Zealand.

A Quaker, Ruth Morris was active within the Quaker Committee on Jails and Justice (QCJJ, which is now known as Quakers Fostering Justice [QFJ]), the first religious group to take a stand in favor of prison abolition in 1981. She played an important role in the organization of the first International Conference on Penal Abolition (ICOPA) in Toronto in 1983 [see insert on p. 21]. In 1990, she founded Rittenhouse: A New Vision, an organization promoting penal abolition and transformative justice.

(which would be a real regression from feminist advances), but rather that it is dangerous to portray perpetrators as monsters or exceptions. As emphasized by CARA, "If we separate ourselves from the offenders by stigmatizing them, then we fail to see how we contributed to conditions that allow violence to happen."[39]

For this reason, relatives and friends of perpetrators, in particular men, must participate in TJ proceedings.[40] Their role is crucial in helping perpetrators recognize their responsibilities, and accompanying them in their development. This role must not be conceived in terms of "loyalty" (toward a perpetrator *versus* a victim), but rather as a part of the collective accountability incumbent upon them.

Education and Limits

TJ practices face many challenges.[41] First off, they are based on the goodwill of perpetrators, who must recognize the harm that has been caused and agree to commit to the work of TJ in order to help transform the problematic situation. Furthermore, not all victims have the same level of access to community resources—access is sometimes proportional to their involvement in activist and community networks and can go hand in hand with "activist capital." In other words, it is sometimes difficult to extricate TJ practices from affinity groups. In addition, because TJ practices do not delegate the work of resolving problematic situations to professionals, they demand a lot of time, and women and LGBTQ people tend to invest themselves (in all the senses of the term) much more than others. Finally, because of the limits of community resources (which are the resources of the people involved), TJ practices are sometimes impoverished when it comes to complex situations, notably in the most serious cases of physical violence.

The development of TJ does not guarantee the future abolition of the criminal justice system. It is nevertheless, as of today, necessary for communities that are most impacted by the criminal justice system's existence. Like restorative justice, TJ risks being appropriated by the state, even if that goes against the spirit in which it was conceived. The Canadian state was a pioneer in terms of co-opting restorative justice, having established, in the 1990s, healing circles and sentencing circles (see insert below). In France, the "Taubira law," passed on August 15, 2004, provided for the development of programs based on the Canadian model of victim-prisoner meetings. These meetings, between those who have suffered sexual harm during their childhood and people convicted for this kind of offense, are meant to help the former to better understand the incidents (part of the needs of victims; see chapter 2), but also to help convicted people to recognize their responsibility in the harm caused. Although there is no doubt surrounding the benefits

---

Sentencing Circles and Healing Lodges

Sentencing circles and healing lodges for Indigenous people were developed in Canada in the 1990s.[42] At the same time, Australia and New Zealand established community conferences, originally intended for minors.

In addition to offenders and victims, members of communities participate in these proceedings. Depending on the program, these might be lawyers, educators, law enforcement officers, family members, etc. The proceedings begin with narratives that each participant gives, explaining their actions or the harm suffered, and offering suggestions for remedying it. Then an agreement is passed among everyone present. This agreement can be presented to a court, either to be considered during sentencing, or to be substituted partially or entirely for a sentence.

These programs reproduce certain cultural functions and practices that various Indigenous peoples in these countries have developed, and are based "on principles of mediation operations."[43] They aim to reduce the proportion of criminalized people within Indigenous populations.

---

that might be derived for the people who participate in these meetings, there is reason to worry about the ways that criminal justice policies co-opt techniques conceived explicitly outside of them.

Constructing Political, Material, and Emotional Solidarities

The development of TJ practices allows for collective freedom from the criminal justice system, but the construction of political, material, and emotional solidarity between everyone affected by its existence is also necessary for the advancement of penal abolitionism.

The Charity Trap

When confronted with the criminal justice system, whether as a victim or as a criminalized individual, or through our criminalized friends or relatives, there are often interactions with certain organizations: legal aid, various support groups (prison education and visitation support programs), etc. But the development of the nonprofit-industrial complex (see chapter 4) is not unrelated to the "industrialization of domestic violence intervention" described by Kimberlé W. Crenshaw.[44] The evolution of this connection constitutes, in my view, one of the greatest contemporary challenges that the abolitionist movement must combat: focusing on prison or on the criminal justice system risks ignoring the other ways in which our problems are being "taken over" by people other than ourselves.

The nonprofit sector benefits (financially and morally) from the existence of the criminal justice system, and from the lives of the people who are confronted by it. Prisoners, those who are released from prison, or who have friends or relatives in prison constitute, for them, sources of employment and moral satisfaction (typical in charitable work, whether it is voluntary or paid). Just as social workers depend on prisoners and their friends or relatives for their funding and employment, the volunteer and charitable sector justifies its existence and its funding by defining the people that it "takes responsibility for" in terms of their problems (domestic, family, etc.) and their deficiencies (of education, of know-how, etc.). Contrary to what this suggests, incarcerated women are not in fact bad mothers, men in prison are not violent husbands and alcoholics, and having an incarcerated husband does not guarantee domestic problems or a lack of proper care for children. Incarcerated people and their relatives and loved ones must not be pathologized by the volunteer and charity sector. This violates our dignity and contributes to making women, the poorest populations, and people of color the political targets of social control under the guise of charity.

Furthermore, this sector claims to respond to the needs (maintenance of family bonds, care of children, etc.) of people "under their responsibility," even though it is a cog in the system that created these needs. These people are at risk of becoming captives of this sector's "benevolence" and the dependence it establishes among its "beneficiaries." We need to learn to think collectively, to construct our autonomy, and to take stock of our strengths and knowledge. Personally, participating in the creation of a guide for relatives and friends of prisoners allowed me to understand the amount of knowledge that I had acquired while supporting relatives and friends of prisoners.[45] We need more tools (such as guides, online discussion forums, gathering places, etc.) to help freely share this knowledge. The nonprofit sector must not be allowed to appropriate them, for example, by offering (and then commercializing) services and knowledge that are already being exchanged freely among people confronted by the criminal justice system.

The expansion of the charitable and volunteer sector is accompanied by a broader "NGO-ization"[46] movement of all left struggles—feminist struggles and struggles in and around prison alike. For a few decades now, NGOs and other organizations, overseen by "specialists" considered legitimate intermediaries by the state, have been slowly eclipsing activist struggles and work conducted by people directly involved in the harms they combat. As a whole, the volunteer and non-profit sector, despite its progressive ambitions, only serves to contribute to the perpetuation of these problems because it neither challenges the system itself nor the way it affects our lives. In sum, there is infinitely less need for its charity and expertise than for collective struggles.

Inclusivity or Solidarity?

Feminist and queer abolitionism is not an abolitionism that "includes" women and LGBTQ people or renders them "visible." It is not about "inclusivity" or "visibility." These are buzz words, and the real question is that of power within the abolitionist movement, both on the theoretical level (how is the situation of women and LGBTQ people integrated into the critical analysis of the criminal justice system?) and on the collective level (what roles do women and LGBTQ people occupy in the struggle?). Abolitionism must be feminist and queer, by incorporating feminist and queer analyses and by providing solutions to the large-scale victimhood of women and LGBTQ people, as well as to the forms of criminalization they suffer.

Rather than thinking in terms of "visibility" and "inclusivity," it seems more pertinent to me to explore how we can build solidarity. This is because I have rarely observed abolitionist groups that take the specific logistical constraints of women and, in particular, those who have relatives and friends in prison, into account. In the first political group I participated in, I had to raise what seemed to me an obvious issue: the meetings were being held on the day of the week when the majority of visits took place. More generally, the "triple shift"[47] shouldered by women who are politically involved (in the abolitionist fight or otherwise) is rarely taken into account. If solidarity is to be built, it is necessary not only for everyone to be able to engage politically, but also that these engagements be incorporated into people's lives. As emphasized by Julia Sudbury, the abolitionist fight cannot be detached from our emotional—or material—needs.[48]

In the Shadows of Walls and Men

Chapter 4 explored the material and emotional conditions that many relatives and friends of prisoners endure, along with the vulnerability linked to this status, which creates certain obstacles to their political engagement, especially in abolitionist movements. These movements should take these obstacles seriously by fostering, without being patronizing, the creation of solidarity (material and emotional) between relatives and friends of prisoners.

I will not detail what it would mean to concretely place relatives and friends of prisoners at the center of the abolitionist movement. This work must be undertaken collectively. As a prerequisite, however, it must be recognized that relatives and loved ones of prisoners serve their own sentences, sentences not handed down by judges, but which have material, financial, and emotional dimensions. Abolitionist struggles rather naturally incorporate the demands of prisoners, including struggles over living conditions and whether or not they might be reformist in nature. Recognizing the sentences served by their relatives and friends must translate into the recognition of their demands as well—even if these demands might be deemed reformist by some activists.

A person supporting a gravely ill loved one generally elicits a form of respect. But supporting a loved one in prison demands at least as much moral and emotional investment—not to mention a great deal of know-how (for example, in terms of organization). Unfortunately, shame is more common than pride for friends or relatives, especially for women—while men who are released from prison sometimes enjoy a certain prestige. Abolitionist movements must help combat this shame.

I am calling for the building of solidarity and empowerment, though without suggesting that creating autonomous groups of relatives and friends of prisoners is a useful strategy in the current context. Such groups (like prisoners' unions)[49] tend rather naturally to position themselves in the judicial sphere. They also tend to rapidly succumb to individual quarrels because they are based on affinities. I have observed these pitfalls many times over the course of the last fifteen years, in France and elsewhere.

Advocating for relatives and friends of prisoners is not without risk. Embraced without precaution (in particular from the "women and children" angle), these efforts risk contributing to the innocentist tendency of abolitionism.[50] To present relatives and friends of prisoners as "innocent" reinforces the idea that there are in fact "guilty" and "innocent" people, and the legitimate existence of prison is tied to this notion. Innocentism is all the more dangerous because it generally goes hand in hand with judiciarism, which is often embraced by people confident in their rights and who are able, because of their social position, to exercise them. Innocentism and judiciarism, distinguishing between the "guilty" and the "innocent," and positioning themselves in the domain of "rights," are, in my view, two pitfalls to avoid. They do not challenge the existence of prison in any way, and the critiques they make of prison are perfectly compatible with legitimist discourse.

Constructing political, material, and emotional solidarity between relatives and friends of prisoners must contribute to our empowerment as women. We cannot, in my view, think of relatives and friends without reflecting from a feminist perspective on the fact that women whose relatives and friends are incarcerated are, on the whole, dependent and vulnerable, notably because they continue to do domestic work, which is undeniably disjointed and done from a distance. It's possible to make this observation without abandoning profound empathy for incarcerated men: the forms of dispossession they endure *inside* are not dissimilar to the forms of long-distance control some of them impose on partners and loved ones' domestic work, as a way of maintaining something resembling a life *outside*.

The task of building solidarity among relatives and friends of prisoners is not without obstacles, beginning with the ways in which the social relationships among incarcerated men influence those among the relatives and friends of prisoners. No one understands better than we do that on the way to visiting rooms, we are not to disturb the laws of men and the relationships that they have chosen for themselves. We have to build solidarity among ourselves, *outside*, that is freed from the power relations that exist *inside,* among prisoners.

To emancipate ourselves from carceral hierarchies and from those based on the offenses for which our relatives and friends are incarcerated also means being careful not to reproduce the individualism that prison creates. We must walk a narrow path, between our emancipation as relatives and friends and as women (by building social relationships and struggles outside of those organized and structured by men), all while respecting the fragile equilibrium that exists on the inside.

Epilogue

Because penal abolition can only be "unfinished,"[1] to borrow an expression from Thomas Mathiesen, we are making our way toward a destination that is somewhat hazy. Our path is similar to all those that must be traveled without a map, a journey where we may be tempted by forks in the road. As we advance along this path, the landscape appears from new angles and sometimes we notice that we have made a wrong turn. For us women, this path is littered with traps: because we are often holding up more than half the sky, because those among us who have walked in the shadows of the walls know that the path is long, especially if we carry within ourselves the memories of those who have lost their lives here.

I wrote this book in the way we might stop on the edge of the path: to contemplate the efforts of those who began this journey, and in recognition that we merely continue along the path they forged. I wrote it the way we might place a stone on the path to remember where we have been. I wrote it despite the silences and screams. I wrote it while reminding myself that the work of those who preceded us and whom we carry within us is our strength, and that it grows uncontrollably over the course of our journey. This path will lead us, though not without challenges, toward a world without prison.

I wrote this book for all the women I have walked with for part of the way and for those with whom I have only crossed paths. I would not have been able to write it without you all. Those who have never seen justice, those who are behind the walls, and those who are at the prison gates. All of your doubt, fear, anger, and hope give my heart its purpose, which is to beat against all prisons.

Acknowledgments

Thank you to my editor, Marie-Eve Lamy, for her enthusiasm and confidence which have allowed for this book to come to fruition. The writing of *Free Them All* owes a lot to the encouragement of friends and comrades. Warm thanks to Laure, Paula, Emma, Francine, Noémie, Anne, Lydia, Geneviève, and all those with whom I shared parts of the manuscript. Thanks also to Fred, Paulin, Rafik, Romain, and Naima for their support at various moments.

Finally, this book would not exist without the tears that never really dry, the anger against the walls, and the stolen joy. To Fred, who shared all of this with me, and for everything else too.

Bibliography

Adler, Amy, "The Perverse Law of Child Pornography," *Columbia Law Review*, vol. 101, no. 2, 2001.

Adler, Freda, *Sisters in Crime: The Rise of the New Female Criminal*, New York: McGraw-Hill, 1975.

Alexander, Michelle, *The New Jim Crow: Mass Incarceration in the Age of Colorblindness*, New York: The New Press, 2010.

Allard, Sharon Angella, "Rethinking Battered Woman Syndrome: A Black Feminist Perspective," *UCLA Women's Law Journal*, no. 1, 1991.

American Friends Service Committee, *Struggle for Justice: A Report on Crime and Punishment in America*, New York: Hill and Wang, 1971.

Artières, Philippe, Laurent Quero, et Michelle Zancarini-Fournel, *Le Groupe d'information sur les prisons. Archives d'une lutte 1970–1972*, Paris, éd. de l'IMEC, 2003.

Baker, Catherine, *Pourquoi faudrait-il punir? Sur l'abolition du système pénal*, Lyon: Tahin Party, 2004 [1985].

Ball, Matthew, "What's Queer About Queer Criminology?" in Dana Peterson and Vanessa R. Panfil (eds.), *Handbook of LGBT Communities, Crime, and Justice*, New York: Springer, 2014.

Barak, Gregg, *Crimes by the Capitalist State: An Introduction to State Criminality*, Albany: SUNY Press, 1991.

Bassichis, Morgan, *It's War in Here: A Report on the Treatment of Transgender and Intersex People in New York State Men's Prisons*, New York: Sylvia Rivera Law Project, 2007.

—, Alexander Lee and Dean Spade, "Building an Abolitionist Trans and Queer Movement With Everything We've Got," in Eric A. Stanley and Nat Smith (eds.), *Captive Genders: Trans Embodiment and the Prison Industrial Complex*, Oakland: AK Press, 2011.

Beauvoir, Simone de, *Le deuxième sexe*, Paris: Gallimard, 1999 [1949].

Belknap, Joanne, *The Invisible Woman: Gender, Crime, and Justice*, Belmont: Wadsworth, 2001.

Bérard, Jean, *La justice en procès. Les mouvements de contestation face au système pénal (1968–1983)*, Paris: Presses de Sciences Po, 2013.
Bernstein, Elizabeth, "Carceral Politics as Gender Justice? The 'Traffic in Women' and Neoliberal Circuits of Crime, Sex, and Rights," *Theory and Society,* vol. 41, no. 3, 2012.
—, "Militarized Humanitarianism Meets Carceral Feminism: The Politics of Sex, Rights, and Freedom in Contemporary Anti-Trafficking Campaigns," *Signs,* vol. 36, no. 1, 2010.
—, "The Sexual Politics of New Abolitionism," *Differences,* vol. 18, no. 3, 2007.
Blais, Mélissa et Francis Dupuis-Déri, *Le mouvement masculiniste au Québec: l'antiféminisme démasqué,* Montréal: Remue-ménage, 2015.
Boutilier, Sophia and Lana Wells, *The Case for Reparative and Transformative Justice Approaches to Sexual Violence in Canada: A Proposal to Pilot and Test New Approaches,* Calgary: University of Calgary/Shift: The Project to End Domestic Violence, 2018.
Braithwaite, John, "Challenging Just Deserts: Punishing White-Collar Criminals," *The Journal of Criminal Law and Criminology,* vol. 73, no. 2, 1982.
—, *Crime, Shame and Reintegration,* Cambridge: Cambridge University Press, 1989.
Braz, Rose, "Kinder, Gentler, Gender Responsive Cages: Prison Expansion Is Not Prison Reform," in Russell Immarigeon (ed.), *Women and Girls in the Criminal Justice System: Policy Issues and Practice Strategies,* vol. 2, Kingston, NJ: Civic Research Institute, 2006.
Brazzell, Melanie, "Wasmacht uns sicher? Die Polizei jedenfalls nicht der Transformative-Justice-Ansatz," *Analyse & Kritik,* no. 621, 2016.
Brossat, Alain, *Pour en finir avec la prison,* Paris: La Fabrique, 2001.
Brownmiller, Susan, *Le viol,* Paris: Stock, 1976 [1975].
Buck, Marilyn and Laura Whitehorn, "Cruel but Not Unusual: The Punishment of Women in US Prisons," in Joy James (ed.), *The New Abolitionists: Neo-slave Narratives and Contemporary Prison Writings,* Albany: SUNY Press, 2005.
Bumiller, Kristin, *In an Abusive State: How Neoliberalism Appropriated the Feminist Movement Against Sexual Violence,* Durham, NC: Duke University Press, 2008.
Burdon, William M. and Catherine A. Gallagher, "Coercion and Sex Offenders: Controlling Sex Offending Behavior Through

Incapacitation and Treatment," *Criminal Justice and Behavior,* no. 2, 2002.

Cantor, James M. and Ian V. McPhail, "Non-Offending Pedophiles," *Current Sexual Health Reports,* vol. 8, no. 3, 2016.

Cardi, Coline, "La déviance des femmes: entre prison, justice et travail social," *Déviance et société,* vol. 31, no. 1, 2007.

—, "Le féminin maternel ou la question du traitement pénal des femmes," *Pouvoirs,* no. 128, 2009.

— et Geneviève Pruvost (eds.), *Penser la violence des femmes,* Paris: La Découverte, 2012.

Carlen, Pat, *Alternatives to Women's Imprisonment,* Milton Keynes: Open University Press, 1990.

Carrier, Nicolas et Justin Piché, "Actualité de l'abolitionnisme," *Champ pénal/Penal Field,* vol. 12, 2015.

Chandler, Cynthia, "The Gender-Responsive Prison Expansion Movement," in Rickie Solinger *et al.* (eds.), *Interrupted Life: Experiences of Incarcerated Women in the United States,* Berkeley: University of California Press, 2010.

Charbit, Joël et Gwenola Ricordeau, "Au risque de la participation: comparaison des syndicats de prisonniers en France et aux États-Unis," *Participations,* vol. 3, no. 22, 2018.

Chen, Ching-In, Jai Dulani, and Leah Lakshmi Piepzna-Samarasinha, (eds.), *The Revolution Starts at Home: Confronting Intimate Violence Within Activist Communities,* Cambridge: South End Press, 2011.

Chesney-Lind, Meda, "Patriarchy, Crime, and Justice: Feminist Criminology in an Era of Backlash," *Feminist Criminology,* vol. 1, no. 1, 2006.

—, "Patriarchy, Prisons, and Jails: A Critical Look at Trends in Women's Incarceration," *The Prison Journal,* vol. 71, no. 1, 1991.

— and Kathleen Daly, "Feminism and Criminology," *Justice Quarterly,* vol. 5, no. 4, 1988.

— and Marc Mauer, *Invisible Punishment: The Collateral Consequences of Mass Imprisonment,* New York: The New Press, 2002.

— and Noelie Rodriguez, "Women Under Lock and Key: A View From the Inside," *The Prison Journal,* vol. 63, no. 2, 1983.

— and Randall G. Shelden, *Girls, Delinquency, and Juvenile Justice,* London: Wiley, 2014 [1992].

Christie, Nils, "Conflicts as Property," *British Journal of Criminology,* vol. 17, no. 1, 1977.

—, "The Ideal Victim," in Ezzat A. Fattah (ed.), *From Crime Policy to Victim Policy: Reorienting the Justice System*, London: Palgrave Macmillan, 1986.

—, *L'industrie de la punition. Prison et politique pénale en Occident*, Paris: Autrement, coll. "Frontières," 2003 [1993].

Chrysalis Collective, "Beautiful, Difficult, Powerful: Ending Sexual Assault Through Transformative Justice," in Ching-In Chen, Jai Dulani, and Leah Lakshmi Piepzna-Samarasinha (eds.), *The Revolution Starts at Home: Confronting Intimate Violence Within Activist Communities*, Cambridge: South End Press, 2011.

Collectif, *Réflexions autour d'un tabou. L'infanticide*, Paris: Cambourakis, coll. "Sorcières," 2015.

Collins, Patricia Hills, *Black Feminist Thought*, London: Routledge, 2009 [2000].

Comfort, Megan, "'C'est plein de mecs bien en taule!' Incarcération de masse aux États-Unis et ambivalence des épouses," *Actes de la recherche en sciences sociales*, vol. 4, no. 169, 2007.

—, *Doing Time Together: Love and Family in the Shadow of the Prison*, Chicago: University of Chicago Press, 2008.

Communities Against Rape and Abuse (CARA), "Taking Risks: Implementing Grassroots Community Accountability Strategies," in Incite!, *The Revolution Will Not Be Funded: Beyond the Non-Profit Industrial Complex*, Cambridge: South End Press, 2006.

Conrad, Ryan, *Against Equality: Prisons Will Not Protect You*, Lewiston, ME: Against Equality Press, 2012.

Conroy, Shana et Adam Cotter, "Les agressions sexuelles autodéclarées au Canada, 2014," *Juristat*, Ottawa: Statistique Canada, 2017.

Cook, Sandy and Suzanne Davies, *Harsh Punishment: International Experiences of Women's Imprisonment*, Boston: Northeastern University Press, 1999.

Corrigan, Rose, "Making Meaning of Megan's Law," *Law & Social Inquiry*, vol. 31, no. 2, 2006.

Cotter, Adam, *La victimisation avec violence chez les femmes ayant une incapacité*, Ottawa: Statistique Canada, 2014.

CR10 Publication Collective, *Abolition Now! Ten Years of Strategy and Struggle Against the Prison Industrial Complex*, Oakland: AK Press, 2008.

Creative Interventions, *Creative Interventions Toolkit: A Practical Guide to Stop Interpersonal Violence*, 2012.

Crenshaw, Kimberlé W., "From Private Violence to Mass Incarceration: Thinking Intersectionally About Women, Race, and Social Control," *UCLA Law Review*, vol. 59, no. 6, 2012.

Crew, B.K., "Sex Differences in Patriarchy: Chivalry or Patriarchy?," *Justice Quarterly,* vol. 8, no. 1, 1991.

Darley, Mathilde et Gwénaëlle Mainsant, "Police du genre," *Genèses,* no. 97, 2014.

Davis, Angela, *Autobiographie,* Brussels: Aden, 2013 [1975].

—, "Joan Little: The Dialectics of Rape," *Ms. Magazine,* vol. 3, no. 12, june 1975.

—, *Femmes, race et classe,* Paris: Des femmes – Antoinette Fouque, 2013 [1981].

—, *La prison est-elle obsolète?,* Paris: Au diable vauvert, 2014 [2003].

de Haan, Willem, "Redresser les torts: l'abolitionnisme et le contrôle de la criminalité," *Criminologie,* vol. 25, no. 2, 1992.

Debauche, Alice *et al., Enquête Virage et premiers résultats sur les violences sexuelles,* Paris: INED, 2017.

Delisle, Claire *et al.,* "The International Conference on Penal Abolition (ICOPA): Exploring Dynamics and Controversies as Observed at ICOPA 15 on Algonquin Territory," *Champ pénal/Penal Field,* vol. 12, 2015.

Delphy, Christine (ed.), *Un troussage de domestique,* Paris: Syllepse, coll. "Nouvelles questions féministes," 2011.

Donzelot, Jacques, *La police des familles,* Paris: Éditions de Minuit, coll. "Reprise," 2005 [1977].

Dorlin, Elsa, *Se défendre. Une philosophie de la violence,* Paris: La Découverte, coll. "Zones," 2017.

Durazo, Ana Clarissa Rojas, Alisa Bierria, and Mimi Kim (eds.), "Community Accountability: Emerging Movements to Transform Violence," *Social Justice, Conflict & World Order,* vol. 37, no. 4, 2012.

Durkheim, Émile, *Les règles de la méthode sociologique,* Paris: Presses universitaires de France, coll. "Quadrige," 1993 [1895].

Elliott, Ian A. and Gary Zajac, "The Implementation of Circles of Support and Accountability in the United States," *Aggression and Violent Behavior,* vol. 25, 2015.

Faith, Karlene, "Aboriginal Women's Healing Lodge: Challenge to Penal Correctionalism?," *Journal of Human Justice,* vol. 6, no. 2, 1995.

—, "La résistance à la pénalité: un impératif féministe," *Criminologie,* vol. 35, no. 2, 2002.

Farr, Kathryn Ann, "Defeminising and Dehumanising Female Murderers: Depictions of Lesbians on Death Row," *Women and Criminal Justice,* vol. 11, no. 1, 2000.

Fattah, Ezzat A., "Quand la recherche et le savoir scientifique cèdent le pas à l'activisme et au parti pris," *Criminologie*, vol. 43, no. 2, 2010.

Ferraro, Kathleen J. and Angela M. Moe, "Mothering, Crime and Incarceration," *The Journal of Contemporary Ethnography*, vol. 32, no. 1, 2003.

Fleetwood, Jennifer, *Drug Mules: Women in the International Cocaine Trade*, London: Palgrave Macmillan, 2014.

Foucault, Michel, *Dits et écrits*, t. 2, *1976–1988*, Paris: Gallimard, coll. "Bibliothèque des sciences humaines," 1995.

—, "Préface," in Serge Livrozet, *De la prison à la révolte*, Paris: L'Esprit frappeur, 1999 [1973].

—, *Surveiller et punir. Naissance de la prison*, Paris: Gallimard, coll. "Tel," 1975.

Freedman, Estelle, "The Prison Lesbian. Race, Class and the Construction of the Aggressive Female Homosexual," *Feminist Studies*, vol. 22, no. 2, 1996.

—, *Their Sisters Keepers: Women's Prison Reform in America, 1830–1930*, Ann Arbor: University of Michigan Press, 1981.

Frigon, Sylvie, "La création de choix pour les femmes incarcérées: sur les traces du groupe d'étude sur les femmes purgeant une peine fédérale et de ses conséquences," *Criminologie*, vol. 35, no. 2, 2002.

generationFIVE, *Toward Transformative Justice. A Liberatory Approach to Child Sexual Abuse and Other Forms of Intimate and Community Violence*, 2007, criticalresistance.org.

Gerber, Jurg and Susan L. Weeks, "Women as Victims of Corporate Crime: A Call for Research on a Neglected Topic," *Deviant Behavior*, vol. 13, no. 4, 1992.

Giallombardo, Rose, *Society of Women. A Study of a Women's Prison*, New York: John Wiley & Sons, 1966.

Gillespie, Cynthia K., *Justifiable Homicide: Battered Women, Self Defense, and the Law*, Columbus: Ohio State University Press, 1990.

Gilmore, Ruth Wilson, *Golden Gulag: Prisons, Surplus, Crisis, and Opposition in Globalizing California*, Berkeley: University of California Press, 2007.

Goffman, Erving, *Stigmate. Les usages sociaux des handicaps*, Paris: Éditions de Minuit, coll. "Le sens commun," 1975 [1963].

Gotell, Lise, "Reassessing the Place of Criminal Law Reform in the Struggle Against Sexual Violence: A Critique of the Critique of

Carceral Feminism," in Anastasia Powell, Nicola Henry, and Asher Flynn (eds.), *Rape Justice: Beyond the Criminal Law,* New York: Palgrave Macmillan, 2015.

Groman, Dvora et Claude Faugeron, "Actualités bibliographiques. La criminalité féminine libérée: de quoi?," *Déviance et société,* vol. 3, no. 4, 1979.

Guenther, Lisa and Chloë Taylor, "Introduction: Queer, Trans, and Feminist Responses to the Prison Nation," *philoSOPHIA,* vol. 6, no. 1, 2016.

Guérin, Anne, *Prisonniers en révolte, quotidien carcéral, mutineries et politique pénitentiaire en France (1970–1980),* Marseille: Agone, coll. "Mémoires sociales," 2013.

Halstead, Imogen, "Does the Custody-Based Intensive Treatment (CUBIT) Program for Sex Offenders Reduce Re-Offending?," *Crime and Justice Bulletin,* Sydney: NSW Bureau of Crime Statistics and Research, no. 193, July 2016.

Hannah-Moffat, Kelly, "Feminine Fortresses: Woman-Centered Prisons?," *The Prison Journal,* vol. 75, no. 2, 1995.

—, *Punishment in Disguise: Penal Governance and Federal Imprisonment of Women in Canada,* Toronto: University of Toronto Press, 2001.

Hannem, Stacey, "Stigma and Marginality: Gendered Experiences of Families of Male Prisoners in Canada," in Aaron Doyle, Dawn Moore (eds.), *Critical Criminology in Canada: New Voices, New Directions,* Vancouver/Toronto: UBC Press, 2011.

— and Louise Leonardi, *Forgotten Victims: The Mental Health and Well-Being of Families Affected by Crime and Incarceration in Canada,* Kingston, Ont.: Canadian Families and Corrections Network, 2015.

Hanson, R. Karl *et al.,* "High-Risk Sex Offenders May Not Be High Risk Forever," *Journal of Interpersonal Violence,* vol. 29, no. 15, 2014.

Harris, M. Kay, "Transformative Justice: The Transformation of Restorative Justice," London: Routledge, 2006.

Heiner, Brady T. and Sarah K. Tyson, "Feminism and the Carceral State: Gender-Responsive Justice, Community Accountability, and the Epistemology of Antiviolence," *Feminist Philosophy Quarterly,* vol. 3, no. 1, 2017.

Hopkins, C. Quince and Mary P. Koss, "Incorporating Feminist Theory and Insights Into a Restorative Justice Response to Sex Offenses," *Violence Against Women,* vol. 11, no. 5, 2005.

Hoppe, Trevor, "Punishing Sex: Sex Offenders and the Missing Punitive Turn in Sexuality Studies," *Law & Social Inquiry,* vol. 41, no. 3, 2016.

Hudson, Barbara, "Restorative Justice and Gendered Violence: Diversion or Effective Justice?," *British Journal of Criminology,* vol. 42, no. 3, 2002.

Hulsman, Louk, "Critical Criminology and the Concept of Crime," *Contemporary Crisis,* vol. 10, no. 1, 1986.

—, "Struggles About Terminology: 'Problematic Situation' vs. 'Crime'," in Yves Cartuyvels *et al.* (eds.), *Politique, police et justice au bord du future: Mélanges pour et avec Lode Van Outrive,* Paris: L'Harmattan, 1998.

— et Jacqueline Bernat de Célis, *Peines perdues. Le système pénal en question,* Paris: Le Centurion, 1982.

Ilea, Adina, "What about 'the Sex Offenders'? Addressing Sexual Harm From an Abolitionist Perspective," *Critical Criminology,* vol. 26, no. 3, 2018.

Incite!, "Gender Violence and the Prison Industrial Complex," in CR10 Publication Collective, *Abolition Now! Ten Years of Strategy and Struggle Against the Prison Industrial Complex,* Oakland: AK Press, 2008 [2001].

—, *The Revolution Will Not Be Funded: Beyond the Non-Profit Industrial Complex,* Cambridge: South End Press, 2007.

INSEE, "L'histoire familiale des hommes détenus," *Synthèses,* no. 59, 2002.

Irvine, Angela, "We've Had Three of Them: Addressing the Invisibility of Lesbian, Gay, Bisexual, and Gender Nonconforming Youths in the Juvenile Justice System," *Columbia Journal of Gender and Law,* vol. 19, no. 3, 2010.

Jaccoud, Mylène, "Les cercles de guérison et les cercles de sentence autochtones au Canada," *Criminologie,* vol. 32, no. 1, 1999.

Jacobsen, Robert, "'Megan's Laws': Reinforcing Old Patterns of Anti-Gay Police Harassment," *Georgetown Law Journal,* vol. 87, no. 7, 1999.

Jashnani, Gaurav, R.J. Maccani, and Alan Greig, "What Does It Feel Like When Change Finally Comes? Male Supremacy, Accountability & Transformative Justice," in Ching-In Chen, Jai Dulani, and Leah Lakshmi Piepzna-Samarasinha (eds.), *The Revolution Starts at Home: Confronting Intimate Violence Within Activist Communities,* Cambridge: South End Press, 2011.

Joël-Lauf, Myriam, "Coûts et bénéfices de l'homosexualité dans les prisons de femmes," *Ethnologie française,* vol. 43, no. 3, 2013.

Johnston, Denise and Megan Sullivan, *Parental Incarceration: Personal Accounts and Developmental Impact,* London: Routledge, 2016.

Kaminski, Dan, "L'éthique du réductionnisme et les solutions de rechange," *Criminologie,* vol. 40, no. 2, 2007.

Katz, Rebecca S. and Hannah M. Willis, "Boys to Offenders: Damaging Masculinity and Traumatic Victimization," in Dale C. Spencer and Sandra Walklate (eds.), *Reconceptualizing Critical Victimology: Interventions and Possibilities,* Lanham: Lexington Books, 2016.

Kim, Mimi, "Moving Beyond Critique: Creative Interventions and Reconstructions of Community Accountability," *Social Justice,* vol. 37, no. 4, 2012.

Knight, Charlotte and Kath Wilson, *LGBT People and the Criminal Justice,* London: Palgrave Macmillan, 2016.

Knopp, Fay Honey, "On Radical Feminism and Abolition," *Peace Review,* vol. 6, no. 2, 1994.

—, *Retraining Adult Sex Abusers: Methods and Models,* Syracuse: Safer Society Press, 1984.

Lancaster, Roger, *Sex Panic and the Punitive State,* Berkeley: University of California Press, 2011.

Lapeyre, Alice, *Flash' Crim,* no. 12, Paris: ONDRP, 2017.

Law, Victoria, *Resistance Behind Bars: The Struggles of Incarcerated Women,* Oakland: PM Press, 2009.

—, "Where Abolition Meets Action: Women Organizing Against Gender Violence," *Contemporary Justice Review,* vol. 14, no. 1, 2011.

Laws, D. Richard and Tony Ward, *Desistance From Sex Offending: Alternatives to Throwing Away the Keys,* New York: The Guilford Press, 2011.

Lawston, Jodie M., *Sisters Outside: Radical Activists Working for Women Prisoners,* Albany: SUNY Press, 2010.

—, " 'We're All Sisters': Bridging and Legitimacy in the Women's Antiprison Movement," *Gender and Society,* vol. 23, no. 5, 2009.

— and Erica R. Meiners, "Ending Our Expertise: Feminists, Scholarship, and Prison Abolition," *Feminist Formations,* vol. 26, no. 2, 2014.

Le Goaziou, Véronique et Laurent Mucchielli, "Les viols jugés en cours d'assises: typologie et variations géographiques," *Questions pénales,* vol. 13, no. 4, 2010.

Le Quéau, Pierre (ed.), *"L'autre peine": Enquête exploratoire sur les conditions de vie des familles de détenus,* Paris: CREDOC, 2000.

Lee, Alexander, "Prickly Coalitions: Moving Prison Abolitionism Forward," in CR10 Publication Collective, *Abolition Now! Ten Years of Strategy and Struggle Against the Prison Industrial Complex,* Oakland: AK Press, 2008.

Lehalle, Sandra (ed.), "Les proches de personnes judiciarisées: expériences humaines et connaissances carcérales," *Criminologie,* vol. 52, no. 1, spring 2019.

Leonard, Elizabeth Dermody, *Convicted Survivors: The Imprisonment of Battered Women Who Kill,* Albany: SUNY Press, 2002.

Light, Miriam, Eli Grant, and Kathryn Hopkins, *Gender Differences in Substance Misuse and Mental Health Amongst Prisoners. Results From the Surveying Prisoner Crime Reduction (SPCR) Longitudinal Cohort Study of Prisoners,* London: Ministry of Justice, 2013.

Livrozet, Annie, *Femme de voyou,* Paris: Lettres libres, 1983.

Loader, Ian, "For Penal Moderation: Notes Towards a Public Philosophy of Punishment," *Theoretical Criminology,* vol. 14, no. 3, 2010.

Löwenbrück, Maël et Louise Viard-Guillot, "Le traitement judiciaire des violences conjugales en 2015," *Infostat Justice,* Paris: Ministry of Justice, no. 159, February 2018.

Lydon, Jason, "A Theology for the Penal Abolition Movement," *Peace Review,* vol. 23, no. 3, 2011.

Lynch, Michael J., "Acknowledging Female Victims of Green Crimes: Environmental Exposure of Women to Industrial Pollutants," *Feminist Criminology,* vol. 13, no. 4, 2017.

MacKenzie, Kaitlin, "'La seule constance... c'est l'inconstance.' Les répercussions des faux positifs des scanneurs à ions sur les familles des détenus canadiens," *Criminologie,* vol. 52, no. 1, spring 2019.

MacLean, Brian D. and Harold E. Pepinsky (eds.), *We Who Would Take No Prisoners: Selections From the Fifth International Conference on Penal Abolition,* Vancouver: Collective Press, 1993.

Mahony, Tina Hotton, Joanna Jacob, and Heather Hobson, *Les femmes et le système de justice pénale,* Ottawa: Statistique Canada, 2017.

Maksymowicz, Duszka, *Femme de parloir,* Paris: L'Esprit frappeur, 2000.

Malakieh, Jamil, *Statistiques sur les services correctionnels pour les adultes et les jeunes au Canada, 2016–2017,* Ottawa: Statistique Canada, 2018.

Maruri, Silpa, "Hormone Therapy for Inmates: A Metonym for Transgender Rights," *Cornell Journal of Law and Public Policy,* vol. 20, no. 3, 2010.

Mathiesen, Thomas, *The Politics of Abolition Revisited*, London: Routledge, 2015 [1974].

Matsunaga, Jennifer, "Two Faces of Transitional Justice: Theorizing the Incommensurability of Transitional Justice and Decolonization in Canada," *Decolonization*, vol. 5, no. 1, 2016.

Maynard, Robyn, *NoirEs sous surveillance. Esclavage, répression et violence d'État au Canada*, Montréal: Mémoire d'encrier, 2018.

Meiners, Erica R., "Never Innocent: Feminist Trouble With Sex Offender Registries and Protection in a Prison Nation," *Meridians*, vol. 9, no. 2, 2009.

Messerschmidt, James W., *Masculinities and Crime: Critique and Reconceptualization of Theory*, Lanham: Rowman & Littlefield Publishers, 1993.

Meyer, Ilan H. *et al.*, "Incarceration Rates and Traits of Sexual Minorities in the United States: National Inmate Survey, 2011–2012," *American Journal of Public Health*, vol. 107, no. 2, 2017.

Mogul, Joey, Andrea Richtie, and Kay Whitlock, *Queer (In)justice: The Criminalization of LGBT People in the United States*, Boston, Beacon Press, 2011.

Morris, Mark (ed.), *Instead of Prisons: A Handbook for Abolitionists*, Syracuse: Prison Research Education Action Project, 1976.

Morris, Ruth, *Penal Abolition: The Practical Choice*, Toronto: Canadian Scholars' Press, 1995.

—, *Stories of Transformative Justice*, Toronto: Canadian Scholars' Press, 2000.

—, "Two Kinds of Victims: Meeting Their Needs," *Journal of Prisoners on Prisons*, vol. 9, no. 2, 1998.

— and Gordon West, (eds.), *The Case for Penal Abolition*, Toronto: Canadian Scholars' Press, 2000.

Nagel, Mechthild, "Trafficking With Abolitionism: An Examination of Anti-Slavery Discourses," *Champ pénal/Penal Field*, vol. 12, 2015.

Nagy, Rosemary L., "The Scope and Bounds of Transitional Justice and the Canadian Truth and Reconciliation Commission," *International Journal of Transitional Justice*, vol. 7, no. 1, 2012.

O'Brien, Patricia, Debora M. Ortega, "Feminist Transformation. Deconstructing Prisons and Reconstructing Justice With Criminalized Women," *Affilia*, vol. 30, no. 2, 2015.

Observatoire national de la délinquance et des réponses pénales (ONDRP), *Éléments de profil des hommes et des femmes de 18 à 75 ans ayant déclaré avoir été victimes de violences physiques ou sexuelles sur deux ans par conjoint cohabitant*, Paris: ONDRP, 2016.

Observatoire national de la violence faite aux femmes, *Lettre no. 12. Violences au sein du couple et violences sexuelles*, Paris: Observatoire national de la violence faite aux femmes, 2017.

Office des Nations Unies contre la drogue et le crime (ONUDC), *Global Study on Homicide 2013: Trends, Contexts, Data*, Vienna, 2013.

Oparah, Julia C., "Feminism and the (Trans)Gender Entrapment of Gender Nonconforming Prisoners," *UCLA Women's Law Journal*, vol. 18, no. 2, 2012.

Ouin, Agnès, "La violence de la justice," *Déviance et société*, vol. 3, no. 1, 1979.

Panfil, Vanessa R., *The Gang's All Queer: The Lives of Gay Gang Members*, New York: NYU Press, 2017.

Parent, Colette, "La contribution féministe à l'étude de la déviance en criminologie," *Criminologie*, vol. 25, no. 2, 1992.

Pepinsky, Harold E., "The Contribution of Feminist Justice to Criminology," *Feminist Teacher*, vol. 4, no. 1, 1989.

— and Richard Quinney, *Criminology as Peacemaking*, Bloomington: Indiana University Press, 1991.

Pheterson, Gail, *Femmes en flagrant délit d'indépendance*, Lyon: Tahin Party, 2010.

Piché, Justin, Shanisse Kleuskens, and Kevin Walby, "The Front and Back Stages of Carceral Expansion Marketing in Canada," *Contemporary Justice Review*, vol. 20, no. 1, 2017.

Piché, Justin and Mike Larsen, "The Moving Targets of Penal Abolitionism ICOPA, Past, Present and Future," *Contemporary Justice Review*, vol. 13, no. 4, 2010.

Pieret, Julien, "Une justice pénale internationale vue par les femmes: continuités et bifurcations dans les analyses féministes de la pénalité," *Champ pénal/Penal Field*, vol. 13, 2016.

Pires, Alvaro, Pierre Landreville, and Victor Blankevoort, "Système pénal et trajectoire sociale," *Déviance et société*, vol. 5, no. 4, 1981.

Pollak, Otto, *The Criminality of Women*, Philadelphia: University of Pennsylvania Press, 1950.

Potter, Hillary, "An Argument for Black Feminist Criminology: Understanding African American Women's Experiences With Intimate Partner Abuse Using an Integrated Approach," *Feminist Criminology*, vol. 1, no. 2, 2006.

Powell, Anastasia, Nicola Henry, and Asher Flynn (eds.), *Rape Justice: Beyond the Criminal Law*, New York: Palgrave Macmillan, 2015.

Pratt, John, *Penal Populism*, New York: Routledge, 2005.

Prison Reform Trust, *"There's a Reason We're in Trouble." Domestic Abuse as a Driver to Women's Offending*, London: Prison Reform Trust, 2017.

Rafter, Nicole Hahn, *Partial Justice: Women in State Prisons, 1800–1935*, Boston: Northeastern University Press, 1985.

Richie, Beth, "A Black Feminist Reflection on the Antiviolence Movement," *Signs*, vol. 25, no. 4, 2000.

—, *Arrested Justice: Black Women, Violence, and America's Prison Nation*, New York: NYU Press, 2012.

—, "Queering Anti-Prison Work: African American Lesbians in the Juvenile Justice System," in Julia Sudbury (ed.), *Global Lockdown: Race, Gender, and the Prison-Industrial Complex*, New York: Routledge, 2005.

Ricordeau, Gwenola, *Les détenus et leurs proches: Solidarités et sentiments à l'ombre des murs*, Paris, Autrement, coll. "Mutations," 2008.

—, "No Abolitionist Movement Without Us! Manifesto for Prisoners' Relatives and Friends," in Massimo Pavarini and Livio Ferrari (eds.), *No Prison*, London: EG Press, 2018.

—, "Sexualités féminines en prison: pratiques, discours et représentations," *Genre, sexualité et société*, no. 1, 2009.

— and Régis Schlagdenhauffen (eds.), "Sexualités et institutions pénales," *Champ pénal/Penal Field*, vol. 13, 2016.

Romito, Patrizia, *Un silence de mortes: La violence masculine occultée*, Paris: Syllepse, coll. "Nouvelles questions féministes," 2006.

Rostaing, Corinne, *La relation carcérale: Identités et rapports sociaux dans les prisons de femmes*, Paris: Presses universitaires de France, coll. "Le lien social," 1997.

—, "L'invisibilisation des femmes dans les recherches sur la prison," *Les Cahiers de Framespa*, no. 25, 2017.

Ryan, Mick, *The Acceptable Pressure Group: Inequality in the Penal Lobby, a Case Study of RAP and the Howard League*, Farnborough: Saxon House, 1978.

Saada Saar, Malika *et al.*, *The Sexual Abuse to Prison Pipeline: The Girls' Story*, Georgetown/Washington: Center for Poverty and Inequality/Georgetown University Law Center, 2015.

Salas, Denis, *La volonté de punir: Essai sur le populisme pénal*, Paris: Hachette, coll. "Pluriel," 2005.

Saleh-Hanna, Viviane, "Black Feminist Hauntology," *Champ pénal/Penal Field*, vol. 12, 2015.

Salle, Grégory, "Situations(s) carcérale(s) en Allemagne. Prison et politique," *Déviance et société*, vol. 27, no. 4, 2003.

Scherr, Mickaël et Aurélien Langlade, "Les caractéristiques des homicides commis à Paris et petite couronne," *Grand Angle*, no. 35, Paris, INHESJ, 2014.

Schwartz, Martin D., "Series Wife Battering Victimizations in the National Crime Survey," *International Journal of Sociology of the Family*, vol. 19, no. 2, 1989.

— and Walter S. De Keseredy, "Left Realist Criminology: Strengths, Weaknesses and the Feminist Critique," *Crime, Law and Social Change*, vol. 15, no. 1, 1991.

Service correctionnel du Canada, *La création de choix: rapport du groupe d'étude sur les femmes purgeant une peine fédérale*, Ottawa: Ministère des Approvisionnements et Services, 1990.

Sexton, Lori, Val Jenness, and Jennifer Sumner, "Where the Margins Meet: A Demographic Assessment of Transgender Inmates in Men's Prisons," *Justice Quarterly*, vol. 27, no. 6, 2010.

Sim, Joe, "The Abolitionist Approach: A British Perspective," in Antony Duff *et al.* (eds.), *Penal Theory and Practice: Tradition and Innovation in Criminal Justice*, Manchester: Manchester University Press, 1994.

Slingeneyer, Thibaut, "La pensée abolitionniste hulsmanienne," Archives de politique criminelle, vol. 27, no. 1, 2005.

Smith, Allison, "Stories of os: Transgender Women: Monstrous Bodies, and the Canadian Prison System," *Dalhousie Journal of Legal Studies*, vol. 23, 2014.

Soledad et associé-e-s, *Guide à l'usage des proches de personnes incarcérées*, 2013.

Soulié, Christophe, *Liberté sur paroles: contribution à l'histoire du Comité d'action des prisonniers*, Bordeaux: Analis, 1995.

Spencer, Dale, "Sex Offender as Homo Sacer," *Punishment & Society*, vol. 11, no. 2, 2009.

Stanley, Eric A. and Nat Smith (eds.), *Captive Genders: Trans Embodiment and the Prison Industrial Complex*, Oakland: AK Press, 2011.

Stanley, Eric, Dean Spade, and Queer (In)Justice, "Queering Prison Abolition, Now?," *American Quarterly*, vol. 64, no. 1, 2012.

Steinert, Heinz, "Beyond Crime and Punishment," *Contemporary Crises*, vol. 10, no. 1, 1986.

Strega, Susan *et al.*, "Never Innocent Victims: Street Sex Workers in Canadian Print Media," *Violence Against Women*, vol. 20, no. 1, 2014.

Strimelle, Véronique, "La justice restaurative: une innovation du pénal?," *Champ pénal/Penal Field*, vol. 5, 2007.

Stubbs, Julie, "Domestic Violence and Women's Safety: Feminist Challenges to Restorative Justice," in Heather Strang et John Braithwaite (eds.), *Restorative Justice and Family Violence*, Cambridge: Cambridge University Press, 2002.

Sudbury, Julia, "Building a Movement to Abolish Prisons: Lessons from the U.S.," *Journal of Prisoners on Prisons*, vol. 18, nos. 1–2, 2009.

—, "From Women Prisoners to People in Women's Prisons: Challenging the Gender Binary in Antiprison Work," in Jodie M. Lawston and Ashley E. Lucas (eds.), *Razor Wire Women: Prisoners, Activists, Scholars, and Artists*, Albany: SUNY Press, 2011.

Szockyj, Elizabeth and James G. Fox (eds.), *Corporate Victimization of Women*, Boston: Northeastern University Press, 1996.

Taylor, Chloë, "Anti-Carceral Feminism and Sexual Assault—a Defense: A Critique of the Critique of the Critique of Carceral Feminism," *Social Philosophy Today*, vol. 34, 2018.

Tjaden, Patricia and Nancy Thoennes, "Prevalence and Consequences of Male-to-Female and Female-to-Male Partner Violence as Measured by the National Violence against Women Survey," *Violence Against Women*, vol. 6, no. 2, 2000.

Thuma, Emily, "Lessons in Self-Defense: Gender Violence, Racial Criminalization, and Anticarceral Feminism," *Women's Studies Quarterly*, vol. 43, nos. 3–4, 2015.

Touraut, Caroline, *La famille à l'épreuve de la prison*, Paris: Presses universitaires de France, coll. "Le lien social," 2012.

Vacheret, Marion, "Les visites familiales privées au Canada, entre réinsertion et contrôle accru: portrait d'un système," *Champ pénal/Penal Field*, vol. 2, 2005.

van Swaaningen, René, *Critical Criminology: Visions From Europe*, London: Sage, 1997.

—, "Feminism and Abolitionism as Critiques of Criminology," *International Journal of the Sociology of Law*, vol. 17, no. 3, 1989.

Vuattoux, Arthur, "*Gender and Judging*, ou le droit à l'épreuve des études de genre," *Tracés*, no. 27, 2014.

—, "Les jeunes Roumaines sont des garçons comme les autres," *Plein droit*, no. 104, 2015.

Wacquant, Loïc, *Les prisons de la misère*, Paris: Raisons d'agir, coll. "Raison d'agir," 1999.

Walker, Lenore, *The Battered Woman*, New York: William Morrow Paperbacks, 1989.

Walter, Emmanuelle, *Sœurs volées: Enquête sur un féminicide au Canada*, Montréal: Lux, 2014.

Whalley, Elizabeth and Colleen Hackett, "Carceral Feminisms: The Abolitionist Project and Undoing Dominant Feminisms," *Contemporary Justice Review*, vol. 20, no. 4, 2017.

Whately, Mark A., "Victim Characteristics Influencing Attributions of Responsibility to Rape Victims: A Meta-Analysis," *Aggression and Violent Behavior*, vol. 1, no. 2, 1996.

Wilson, Robin J., Franca Cortoni and Andrew J. McWhinnie, "Circles of Support & Accountability: A Canadian National Replication of Outcome Findings," *Sexual Abuse*, vol. 21, no. 4, 2009.

Withers, A.J., *Transformative Justice and/as Harm*, Toronto: Rebuild Printing, 2014.

Withers, Lloyd and Jean Folsom, *Incarcerated Fathers: A Descriptive Analysis*, Ottawa: Service correctionnel Canada, 2007.

Woods, Jordan Blair, "'Queering Criminology': Overview of the State of the Field," in Dana Peterson and Vanessa R. Panfil (eds.), *Handbook of LGBT Communities, Crime, and Justice*, New York: Springer, 2014.

World Health Organization (WHO), *Global and Regional Estimates of Violence Against Women: Prevalence and Health Effects of Intimate Partner Violence and Non-Partner Sexual Violence*, 2013, who. int.

Zehr, Howard, *Changing Lenses: A New Focus for Crime and Justice*, Scottdale, PA: Herald Press, 1990.

Additional Resources

This selection of texts (easily available, and rather accessible) and sites allows for a deepening of various theoretical and practical aspects of abolition feminism and, more generally, penal abolitionism.

Readings (In French)

Bérard, Jean, *La justice en procès. Les mouvements de contestation face au système pénal (1968–1983)*, Paris: Presses de Sciences Po, 2013.

Brossat, Alain, *Pour en finir avec la prison*, Paris: La Fabrique, 2001.

"Les Enrageuses, Lavomatic. Lave ton linge en public," 2009, info kiosques.net.

Guérin, Anne, *Prisonniers en révolte, quotidien carcéral, mutineries et politique pénitentiaire en France (1970–1980)*, Marseille: Agone, coll. "Mémoires sociales," 2013.

"Soledad et associées, En finir avec le placard," Recueil de textes de prisonnier.ère.s politiques LGBT, 2015, infokiosques.net.

Readings (In English)

Baker, Catherine, *Against Prisons*, Portland: Microcosm Publishing, 2020.

Carrier, Nicolas and Justin Piché (eds.), "Abolitionnisme – Abolitionism," *Champ pénal/Penal Field*, vol. 12, 2015.

Christie, Nils, *Crime Control as Industry*, New York: Routledge, 2017.

CR10 Publication Collective, *Abolition Now! Ten Years of Strategy and Struggle against the Prison Industrial Complex*, Oakland: AK Press, 2008 [2001].

Davis, Angela Y., *Are Prisons Obsolete?*, New York: Seven Stories Press, 2003.

Gilmore, Ruth Wilson, *Golden Gulag: Prisons, Surplus, Crisis, and Opposition in Globalizing California*, Berkeley: University of California Press, 2007.

Incite!, The Revolution Will Not Be Funded: Beyond the Non-Profit Industrial Complex, Cambridge, MA: South End Press, 2007.

Law, Victoria, *Resistance Behind Bars: The Struggles of Incarcerated Women*, Oakland: PM Press, 2009.

Mathiesen, Thomas, *The Politics of Abolition Revisited*, London: Routledge, 2015 [1974].

Morris, Ruth, *Stories of Transformative Justice*, Toronto: Canadian Scholars' Press, 2000.

Richie, Beth, *Arrested Justice: Black Women, Violence, and America's Prison Nation*, New York: NYU Press, 2012.

Stanley, Eric A. and Nat Smith (eds.), *Captive Genders: Trans Embodiment and the Prison Industrial Complex*, Oakland: AK Press, 2011.

Withers, A.J., *Transformative Justice and/as Harm*, Toronto: Rebuild Printing, 2014.

Sites (France)

Contre tous les lieux d'enfermement: contrelenfermement. noblogs .org.

Désarmons-les!: desarmons.net. Femmes en lutte 93: femmesenlutte93 .over-blog.com.

L'envolée: lenvolee.net.

Sites (Canada)

Cercles de soutien et de responsabilité du Québec: cercledesoutien.org.

Circles of Support and Accountability (COSA): cosacanada.com.

Criminalization and Punishment Education Project (CPEP): cp-ep.org.

End the Prison Industrial Complex (EPIC): epic.noblogs.org.

Journal of Prisoners on Prisons: jpp.org. Mothers Offering Mutual Support (MOMS): momsottawa.com.

Smart Justice Network of Canada: smartjustice.ca.

Tracking the Politics of Criminalization and Punishment in Canada: tpcp-canada.blogspot.com.

Sites (United States)

Creative Interventions: creative-interventions.org.

Critical Resistance: criticalresistance.org.

Survived and Punished: survivedandpunished.org.

Sylvia Rivera Law Project (SRLP): srlp.org.

Notes

Prologue

1 In the original version, the author refers to "Vel d'Hiv," the largest deportation of Jews during the Nazi occupation of France, which took place in July 1942. (NdT)

Introduction

1 Chapter 1 explains precisely what the term "criminal justice" encompasses. For the time being, it can be understood as "pertaining to the judiciary system."

2 I use the term in the political sense that it first had in the United States: the articulation of demands of a queer identity (identity reclaimed by people whose sexuality and/or gender are stigmatized) and of a political struggle against the patriarchy and the oppressions that emerge from norms linked to gender or sexuality. This sense of the word, to evoke a political theory, is different from the use of the word to simply denote an identity.

3 Condemned for the murder of her husband (see page 46), Jacqueline Sauvage received the support of feminist organizations.

4 Notably Gwenola Ricordeau, *Les détenus et leurs proches. Solidarités et sentiments à l'ombre des murs*, Paris: Autrement, "Mutations" series, 2008.

5 Thomas Mathiesen, *The Politics of Abolition Revisited*, London: Routledge, 2015 [1974].

6 Expression to designate people who have been subjected to a criminal proceeding. Its use, like the expression "person in conflict with the criminal justice system," avoids the morally negative connotation associated with the term "convict." It allows the focus to be on the diverse aspects implicated by the confrontation with the judicial system (see chapter 2).

7 All of Us or None is the name of an organization in the United

Stated made up of people who have been incarcerated, who fight against the social exclusion of people released from prison.

8 Adina Ilea, "What about 'the Sex Offenders'? Addressing Sexual Harm from an Abolitionist Perspective," *Critical Criminology*, vol. 26, no. 3, 2018.

9 This expression has already been used in English by abolitionist women: Women Against Prison was the name of a group of women in Michigan in the mid-1970s (we can read about them thanks to the article "Dykes Behind Bars," which they published in 1974 in the first volume of the legendary New York lesbian journal *Dyke*) and by a political group in Australia in the mid-1980s (Sandy Cook and Susanne Davies [ed.], *Harsh Punishment: International Experiences of Women's Imprisonment*, Boston: Northeastern University Press, 1999).

1. Penal Abolitionism

1 The expression "white-collar crime" was created by the US criminologist Edwin H. Sutherland in 1939 and designates "a crime committed by a person of high social status and respectability in the course of his occupation."

2 John Braithwaite, "Challenging Just Deserts: Punishing White-Collar Criminals," *The Journal of Criminal Law and Criminology*, vol. 73, no. 2, 1982.

3 The only work by Louk Hulsman published in France is out of print (Louk Hulsman and Jacqueline Bernat de Celis, *Peines perdues. Le système pénal en question*, Paris: Le Centurion, 1982). For a good summary in French of his theoretical developments, see Thibaut Slingeneyer, "La pensée abolitioniste hulsmanienne," *Archives de politique criminelle*, vol. 27, no. 1, 2005.

4 See Nils Christie, *L'industrie de la punition. Prison et politique pénale en Occident*, Paris: Autrement, "Frontières" series, 2003 [1993].

5 Louk Hulsman, "Critical Criminology and the Concept of Crime," *Contemporary Crisis*, vol. 10, no. 1, 1986.

6 Gregg Barak, *Crimes by the Capitalist State: An Introduction to State Criminality*, Albany: SUNY Press, 1991.

7 Notably Nils Christie, "Conflicts as Property," *British Journal of Criminology*, vol. 17, no. 1, 1977; Hulsman, "Critical Criminology and the Concept of Crime."

8 Heinz Steinert, "Beyond Crime and Punishment," *Contemporary Crises*, vol. 10, no. 1, 1986.

9 Catherine Baker, *Pourquoi faudrait-il punir? Sur l'abolition du système pénal*, Lyon: Tahin Party, 2004 [1985].

10 The term "problematic" applies to situations, but not to behaviors or to people (see chapter 6).

11 See Hulsman, "Critical Criminology and the Concept of Crime."

12 Michel Foucault, *Dits et écrits*, t. 2, 1976–88, Paris: Gallimard, "Bibliothèque des sciences humaines," 1995, p. 796.

13 For such an approach in French, see the work of Alain Brossat, *Pour en finer avec la prison*, Paris: La Fabrique, 2001.

14 Christie, *L'industrie de la punition*, p. 22.

15 An expression designating the structural nature of racism and the way it benefits white people.

16 On contemporary debates within abolitionism, see Nicolas Carrier and Justin Piché, "Actualité de l'abolitionnisme," *Champ pénal/ Penal Field*, vol. 12, 2015.

17 Michel Foucault, *Surveiller et punir. Naissance de la prison*, Paris: Gallimard, "Tel" series, 1975, p. 236.

18 Thomas Mathiesen, *The Politics of Abolition Revisited*, London: Routledge, 2015 [1974].

19 Ezzat A. Fattah, "Quand recherche et savoir scientifique cèdent le pas à l'activisme et au parti pris," *Criminologie*, vol. 43, no. 2, 2010, p. 58.

20 See Rebecca S. Katz and Hannah M. Willis, "Boys to Offenders: Damaging Masculinity and Traumatic Victimization," in Dale C. Spencer and Sandra Walklate (eds.), *Reconceptualizing Critical Victimology: Interventions and Possibilities*, Lanham: Lexington Books, 2016.

21 See cp-ep.org/no-on-prison-expansion-nope-initiative.

22 Long incarcerated during his youth, activist member of the Anarchist Federation and a psychologist, he participates to this day [2019] in the broadcast of the radio show *Ras les murs* (*Tear Down the Walls*) since its creation, to which he contributed, in 1989, on Radio libertaire.

23 See also: Christophe Soulié, *Liberté sur paroles. Contribution à l'histoire du Comité d'action des prisonniers*, Bordeaux: Analis, 1995; Philippe Artières, Laurent Quéro, et Michelle Zancarini-Fournel, *Le Groupe d'information sur les prisons. Archives d'une lutte 1970–1972*, Paris: ed. IMEC, 2003; Anne Guérin, *Prisonniers en révolte. Quotidien carcéral, mutineries et politique pénitentiaire en France (1970–1980)*, Marseille: Agone, "Mémoires sociales" series, 2013; Jean Bérard, *La justice en procès. Les mouvements de contestation face au système pénal (1968–1983)*, Paris: Presses de Sciences Po, 2013.

24 American Friends Service Committee, *Struggle for Justice: A Report on Crime and Punishment in America*, New York: Hill and Wang, 1971.

25 Mark Morris (ed.), *Instead of Prisons: A Handbook for Abolition-ists,* Syracuse: Prison Research Education Action Project, 1976.

26 In particular the text published as a foreword: "Nine Perspectives for Prison Abolitionists."

27 See Justin Piché and Mike Larsen, "The Moving Targets of Penal Abolitionism: ICOPA, Past, Present, and Future," *Contemporary Justice Review,* vol. 13, no. 4, 2010; Claire Delisle, Maria Basualdo, Adina Ilea, and Andrea Hughes, "The International Conference on Penal Abolition (ICOPA): Exploring Dynamics and Controversies as Observed at ICOPA 15 on Algonquin Territory," *Champ pénal/ Penal Field,* vol. 12, 2015.

28 It is nevertheless ironic to note that prison found, at its origins, sources of inspiration in the Christian institution of the monastery and, in particular, in the solitary exercise of prayer.

29 Jason Lydon, "A Theology for the Penal Abolition Movement," *Peace Review: A Journal of Social Justice,* vol. 23, no. 3, September 2011.

30 Since 2005, Critical Resistance (criticalresistance.org) has distrib-uted more than 5,000 copies of *The Abolitionist* (abolitionistpaper. wordpress.com).

31 CR10 Publication Collective, *Abolition Now! Ten Years of Strategy and Struggle Against the Prison Industrial Complex,* Oakland: AK Press, 2008.

32 This expression points to the fivefold increase in the number of people detained between the start of the 1980s and 2010 and, more generally, the important proportion of the total US population (325 million people) who are either detained (2.3 million), on probation (more than 3.5 million), or on parole (nearly 900,000) [2019].

33 Michelle Alexander, *The New Jim Crow: Mass Incarceration in the Age of Colorblindness,* New York: The New Press, 2010.

34 Expression designating the laws, promulgated starting in 1876 by the Southern states, that organized racial segregation in public places and services, and which would not be completely abolished until 1964.

35 Angela Davis, *Are Prisons Obsolete?* New York: Seven Stories, 2003.

36 Ruth Wilson Gilmore, *Golden Gulag: Prisons, Surplus, Crisis, and Opposition in Globalizing California,* Berkeley: University of California Press, 2007.

37 Gender-neutral term designating people with Latin American origins.

38 See chapter 5 as well as Mechthild Nagel, "Trafficking With Abo-litionism: An Examination of Anti-Slavery Discourses," *Champ pénal/Penal Field,* vol. 12, 2015.

39 Mick Ryan, *The Acceptable Pressure Group: Inequality in the Penal Lobby, a Case Study of RAP and the Howard League*, Farnborough: Saxon House, 1978, p. 138.

40 He is mainly known for his involvement with the activists of the Front de Libération du Québec (FLQ).

41 Theorist of the "rupture defense" (the use of a trial to denounce an injustice by the legal system itself), he defended numerous anticolonial activists during the Algerian War of Independence.

42 For example, offenses linked to substance use or sex work.

43 I explore this idea further in chapters 5 and 6.

44 See Ian Loader, "For Penal Moderation: Notes Towards a Public Philosophy of Punishment," *Theoretical Criminology*, vol. 14, no. 3, 2010.

45 See Dan Kaminski, "L'éthique du réductionnisme et les solutions de rechange," *Criminologie*, vol. 40, no. 2, 2007.

46 De Haan, "Redresser les torts."

47 Conceptualized in *Réforme et révolution* (1969) by the French philosopher André Gorz, the expression designates reform "with revolutionary potential," because it is not "bestowed by the central power," but the result of the self-determination of a dominated group that imposes it and controls its execution.

48 Mathiesen, *The Politics of Abolition Revisited*.

49 Davis, *Are Prisons Obsolete?*

50 Alexander Lee, "Prickly Coalitions: Moving Prison Abolitionism Forward," in CR10 Publication Collective, *Abolition Now!*

51 Harold E. Pepinsky and Richard Quinney, *Criminology as Peacemaking*, Bloomington: Indiana University Press, 1991.

52 See René van Swaaningen, *Critical Criminology: Visions From Europe*, London: Sage, 1997.

53 Zemiology is based on a critique of "crime" as the subject of criminology. It studies all forms of "social harm," as suggested by its name (*zemia* means "harm" or "damage" in Ancient Greek).

54 See Gilmore, *Golden Gulag*; Loïc Wacquant, *Les prisons de la misère*, Paris: Raisons d'agir, "Raisons d'agir" series, 1999.

55 Notably in Davis, *Are Prisons Obsolete?*

56 See Christie, *L'industrie de la punition.*

57 For Canada, see Justin Piché, Shanisse Kleuskens, and Kevin Walby, "The Front and Back Stages of Carceral Expansion Marketing in Canada," *Contemporary Justice Review*, vol. 20, no. 1, 2017.

58 Traditionally, the history of feminism is thought of as a succession of three waves: the first, from 1850 to 1945, the second (from the end of the 1960s to the 1970s), which was focused on procreation, contraception, and violence against women, and the third, developed in the 1980s and 1990s.

59 The term "victimhood" describes the act of having undergone harm (physical, psychological, or other attack). The term "victimization" designates, more strictly, the act of having been recognized as a victim.

60 James W. Messerschmidt, *Masculinities and Crime: Critique and Reconceptualization of Theory*, Lanham: Rowman & Littlefield Publishers, 1993.

61 Kathleen Daly and Meda Chesney-Lind, "Feminism and Criminology," *Justice Quarterly*, vol. 5, no. 4, 1988.

62 See Colette Parent, "La contribution féministe à l'étude de la déviance en criminologie," *Criminologie*, vol. 25, no. 2, 1992.

63 The term was popularized by the feminist journalist Susan Faludi with the publication, in 1991, of her book *Backlash: The Undeclared War Against American Women*. It focuses on the backlash, at the end of the 1980s, against the advances obtained in the 1970s by feminist movements.

64 Meda Chesney-Lind, "Patriarchy, Crime, and Justice: Feminist Criminology in an Era of Backlash," *Feminist Criminology*, vol. 1, no. 1, 2006.

65 Hillary Potter, "An Argument for Black Feminist Criminology: Understanding African American Women's Experiences With Intimate Partner Abuse Using an Integrated Approach," *Feminist Criminology*, vol. 1, no. 2, 2006.

66 Julia C. Oparah, "Feminism and the (Trans)Gender Entrapment of Gender Nonconforming Prisoners," *UCLA Women's Law Journal*, vol. 18, no. 2, 2012, p. 242. Her older publications are under the name "Julia Sudbury."

67 These terms describe the focus of analyses on heterosexual or cisgender people, to the detriment of non-heterosexual people and trans or queer people.

68 See Matthew Ball, "What's Queer About Queer Criminology?" in Dana Peterson and Vanessa R. Panfil (eds.), *Handbook of LGBTQ Communities, Crime, and Justice*, New York: Springer, 2014; and Jordan Blair Woods, "'Queering Criminology': Overview of the State of the Field," in ibid.

2. The Treatment of Women Victims by the Criminal Justice System

1 Susan Brownmiller, *Against Our Will: Men, Women, and Rape*, New York: Simon & Schuster, 1975.

2 Patrizia Romito, *A Deafening Silence: Hidden Violence Against Women and Children*, Bristol: Policy Press, 2008.

3 Alice Debauche *et al.*, *Enquête Virage et premiers résultats sur les violences sexuelles*, Paris: INED, 2017.

4 Observatoire national de la violence faite aux femmes, *Lettre no. 12. Violences au sein du couple et violences sexuelles*, Paris: Observatoire national de la violence faite aux femmes, 2017.

5 Shana Conroy and Adam Cotter, "Les agressions sexuelles autodéclarées au Canada, 2014," *Juristat*, Ottawa: Statistique Canada, 2017.

6 OMS, *Global and Regional Estimates of Violence against Women: Prevalence and Health Effects of Intimate Partner Violence and Non-Partner Sexual Violence*, WHO, 2013.

7 Brownmiller, *Against Our Will*.

8 See Jurg Gerber and Susan L. Weeks, "Women as Victims of Corporate Crime: A Call for Research on a Neglected Topic," *Deviant Behavior*, vol. 13, no. 4, 1992; Elizabeth Szockyj and James G. Fox (eds.), *Corporate Victimization of Women*, Boston: Northeastern University Press, 1996.

9 See Michael J. Lynch, "Acknowledging Female Victims of Green Crimes. Environmental Exposure of Women to Industrial Pollutants," *Feminist Criminology*, vol. 13, no. 4, October 2018.

10 Debauche *et al.*, *Enquête Virage et premiers résultats sur les violences sexuelles*.

11 Tina Hotton Mahony, Joanna Jacob and Heather Hobson, *Les femmes et le système de justice pénale*, Ottawa: Statistique Canada, 2017.

12 For example, they represent more than two-thirds of the victims of homicide in the Paris region between 2007 and 2013 (Mikaël Scherr and Aurélien Langlade, "Les caractéristiques des homicides commis à Paris et petite couronne," *Grand Angle*, no. 35, Paris: INHESJ, 2014).

13 Alice Lapeyre, *Flash' Crim*, no. 12, Paris: ONDRP, 2017.

14 ONUDC, *Global Study on Homicide 2013: Trends, Contexts, Data*, Vienna: ONUDC, 2013.

15 Mahony, Jacob and Hobson, *Les femmes et le système de justice pénale*.

16 Martin D. Schwartz, "Series Wife Battering Victimizations in the National Crime Survey," *International Journal of Sociology of the Family*, vol. 19, no. 2, 1989.

17 ONDRP, "Éléments de profil des hommes et des femmes de 18 à 75 ans ayant déclaré avoir été victimes de violences physiques ou sexuelles sur deux ans par conjoint cohabitant," Paris: ONDRP, 2016. For statistics on the victimhood in Canada of women with disabilities, see Adam Cotter, *La victimisation avec violence chez les femmes ayant une incapacité*, Ottawa: Statistique Canada, 2014.

18 ONDRP, "Éléments de profil des hommes et des femmes de 18 à 75 ans ayant déclaré avoir été victimes de violences physiques ou sexuelles sur deux ans par conjoint cohabitant."

19 Davis, *Women, Race and Class.*

20 Christine Delphy (ed.), *Un troussage de domestique*, Paris: Syllepse, "Nouvelles questions féministes" series, 2011.

21 For example, on the representation of violence again women sex workers in the Canadian media, see Susan Strega *et al.*, "Never Innocent Victims: Street Sex Workers in Canadian Print Media," *Violence Against Women*, vol. 20, no. 1, January 2014.

22 Like the opinion column "Nous défendons une liberté d'importuner, indispensable à la liberté sexuelle," signed by a collective of one hundred women (*Le Monde*, January 9, 2018).

23 Observatoire national de la violence faite aux femmes, *Lettre no. 12.*

24 Maël Löwenbrück and Louise Viard-Guillot, "Le traitement judiciaire des violences conjugales en 2015," *Infostat Justice*, Paris: Ministry of Justice, no. 159, February 2018.

25 Conroy and Cotter, "Les agressions sexuelles autodéclarées au Canada, 2014."

26 Patricia Tjaden and Nancy Thoennes, "Prevalence and Consequences of Male-to-Female and Female-to-Male Partner Violence as Measured by the National Violence Against Women Survey," *Violence Against Women*, vol. 6, no. 2, 2000.

27 Research analyzing sentencing and the way in which sentences are decided.

28 See Mark A. Whately, "Victim Characteristics Influencing Attributions of Responsibility to Rape Victims: A Meta-Analysis," *Aggression and Violent Behavior*, vol. 1, no. 2, 1996.

29 Angela Davis, *Women, Race and Class.*

30 See in particular Beth Richie, *Arrested Justice: Black Women, Violence, and America's Prison Nation*, New York: NYU Press, 2012.

31 See the website of the organization Walking With Our Sisters: walking withoursisters.ca.

32 Voir Emmanuelle Walter, *Sœurs volées. Enquête sur un féminicide au Canada*, Montreal: Lux, 2014.

33 The evolution of the number of complaints does not necessarily reflect that of the number of offenses committed. For example, the rise, announced by the Ministry of the Interior, in complaints for rapes and sexual assaults in France in 2017 (respectively 12 percent and 10 percent) is likely explained by the #MeToo movement started in October 2017, which encouraged more women to file complaints.

34 Véronique le Goaziou et Laurent Mucchielli, "Les viols jugés en

cours d'assises: typologie et variations géographiques," *Questions pénales*, vol. 13, no. 4, 2010.

35   For Canada, see Robyn Maynard, *NoirEs sous surveillance. Esclavage, répression, et violence d'État au Canada*, Montreal: Mémoire d'encrier, 2018.

36   Trevor Hoppe, "Punishing Sex: Sex Offenders and the Missing Punitive Turn in Sexuality Studies," *Law & Social Inquiry*, vol. 41, no. 3, 2016.

37   Masculinism is a movement, largely created in response to feminism, which, under the pretext of concern for the masculine condition and the "rights of men," defends male interests and their domination over women. It is much more present in North America than in France, where it is mainly dedicated to the "rights of fathers" (notably SOS Papa). On masculinism in Canada, see Mélissa Blais and Francis Dupuis-Déri (eds.), *Le mouvement masculiniste au Québec. L'antiféminisme démasqué*, Montreal: Remue-ménage, 2015.

38   Just as it would be absurd to demand more male representation among rape victims or those with precarious employment.

39   Arthur Vuattoux, "*Gender and Judging,* ou le droit à l'épreuve des études de genre," *Tracés,* no. 27, 2014.

40   For example, in French criminal law, to be considered recidivism, the perpetrator of an offense punishable by imprisonment of fewer than ten years and more than one year must have been convicted for an offense punished by fewer than ten years of prison committed in the previous five years.

41   Imogen Halstead, "Does the Custody-Based Intensive Treatment (CUBIT) Program for Sex Offenders Reduce Re-Offending?" *Crime and Justice Bulletin,* Sydney: NSW Bureau of Crime Statistics and Research, no. 193, July 2016.

42   Joe Sim, "The Abolitionist Approach: A British Perspective," in Antony Duff *et al.* (eds.), *Penal Theory and Practice: Tradition and Innovation in Criminal Justice,* Manchester: Manchester University Press, 1994.

43   Catherine Baker, *Pourquoi faudrait-il punir? Sur l'abolition du système pénal*, Lyon: Tahin Party, 2004 [1985], p. 18.

44   See Gwenola Ricordeau and Régis Schlagdenhauffen (eds.), "Sexualités et institutions pénales," *Champ pénal/Penal Field,* vol. 13, 2016.

45   James M. Cantor and Ian V. McPhail, "Non-Offending Pedophiles," *Current Sexual Health Reports,* vol. 8, no. 3, 2016.

46   Ibid.

47   Dale Spencer, "Sex Offender as Homo Sacer," *Punishment & Society,* vol. 11, no. 2, 2009.

48 Law no. 2017-258 from February 28, 2017, article 24.

49 Amy Adler, "The Perverse Law of Child Pornography," *Columbia Law Review*, vol. 101, no. 2, 2001.

50 Chloë Taylor, "Anti-Carceral Feminism and Sexual Assault—a Defense: A Critique of the Critique of the Critique of Carceral Feminism," *Social Philosophy Today*, vol. 34, 2018.

51 Notably Anastasia Powell, Nicola Henry, and Asher Flynn (eds.), *Rape Justice: Beyond the Criminal Law*, New York: Palgrave Macmillan, 2015.

52 D. Richard Laws and Tony Ward, *Desistance From Sex Offending: Alternatives to Throwing Away the Keys*, New York: Guilford Press, 2011; R. Karl Hanson, Andrew J.R. Harris, Leslie Helmus, and David Thornton, "High-Risk Sex Offenders May Not Be High Risk Forever," *Journal of Inter-personal Violence*, vol. 29, no. 15, 2014.

53 William M. Burdon and Catherine A. Gallagher, "Coercion and Sex Offenders: Controlling Sex Offending Behavior Through Incapacitation and Treatment," *Criminal Justice and Behavior*, no. 2, 2002.

54 Erica R. Meiners, "Never Innocent: Feminist Trouble With Sex Offender Registries and Protection in a Prison Nation," *Meridians: Feminism, Race, Transnationalism*, vol. 9, no. 2, 2009.

55 For a feminist critique of the categories used by Megan's Laws, see Rose Corrigan, "Making Meaning of Megan's Law," *Law & Social Inquiry*, vol. 31, no. 2, 2006.

56 Research has shown that the criminalization of exposing others to the risk of HIV has no effect on high-risk behavior and can even dissuade people from seeking out screening tests.

57 See Robert Jacobsen, "'Megan's Laws': Reinforcing Old Patterns of Anti-Gay Police Harassment," *Georgetown Law Journal*, vol. 87, no. 7, 1999.

58 This young Black woman was sentenced in Florida in 2012 to twenty years in prison for having shot at her husband who had previously been threatening and violent toward her. Her sentence was subsequently reduced to three years.

59 She was finally released in December 2016, after a presidential pardon given by French president François Hollande.

60 Elizabeth Dermody Leonard, *Convicted Survivors: The Imprisonment of Battered Women Who Kill*, Albany: State University of New York Press, 2002.

61 Lenore E. Walker, *The Battered Woman*, New York: William Morrow Paperbacks, 1980.

62 Cynthia K. Gillespie, *Justifiable Homicide: Battered Women, Self Defense, and the Law*, Columbus: Ohio State University Press, 1990.

63 Brenda Clubine was imprisoned in California in 1983 after the murder of her violent husband and given a minimum sentence of sixteen years. She was released after twenty-six years in prison and continues to fight for the rights of female victims of domestic violence.

64 The so-called "Sin by Silence Bills" refer to the documentary *Sin by Silence* (Olivia Klaus, 2009), which follows the fights led by the CWAA and the experiences of some of its members.

65 She was acquitted in 2012 for the murder of her husband by the Northern Court of Assize.

66 In the Criminal Code, a "state of necessity" allows for an illegal action that prevents an existing or imminent danger, not necessarily linked to an attack (for example, a home invasion to rescue a person).

67 Sharon Angella Allard, "Rethinking Battered Woman Syndrome: A Black Feminist Perspective," *UCLA Women's Law Journal,* vol. 1, 1991.

68 The expression connotes, in the United States, the pressure that African-American women face because of the enduring historical stereotype of the "strong Black woman," wherein they never shirk any form of responsibility (home, work, etc.).

69 Nils Christie, "Conflicts as Property," *British Journal of Criminology,* vol. 17, no. 1, 1977.

70 Ibid.

71 Nils Christie, "The Ideal Victim," in Ezzat A. Fattah (ed.), *From Crime Policy to Victim Policy: Reorienting the Justice System,* London: Palgrave Macmillan, 1986.

72 The body of Alexia Daval was found a few days later and, until his arrest, her husband regularly made public appearances in which he seemed inconsolable.

73 The system of mandatory minimum sentences exists in Canada for certain offenses (such as the sentence of one year of prison for possession of child pornography). Such a mechanism existed in France between 2007 and 2014. It gave, for example, a minimum sentence of four years of prison for the perpetrators of a misdemeanor punishable by ten years in prison.

74 Sentencing guidelines are non-binding rules for judges. However, they are dissuaded from straying from them, even if they are authorized to do so.

75 Expression designating the negative effects, on a victim, resulting from the way in which they are treated.

76 Ruth Morris, "Two Kinds of Victims: Meeting Their Needs," *Journal of Prisoners on Prisons,* vol. 9, no. 2, 1998.

77 Ibid.

78 See Elsa Dorlin, *Self Defense: A Philosophy of Violence*, transl. Kieran Aarons, London: Verso, 2022.

79 Gail Pheterson, *Femmes en flagrant délit d'indépendance*, Lyon: Tahin Party, 2010, p. 58.

3. Criminalized Women

1 Tina Hotton Mahony, Joanna Jacob and Heather Hobson, *Les femmes et le système de justice pénale*, Ottawa: Statistique Canada, 2017.

2 Essentialism presupposes the existence of a nature (or an essence) inherent to beings or things—here, a "feminine nature."

3 Vanessa R. Panfil, *The Gang's All Queer: The Lives of Gay Gang Members*, New York: NYU Press, 2017.

4 Coline Cardi and Geneviève Pruvost (eds.), *Penser la violence des femmes*, Paris: La Découverte, 2012.

5 Freda Adler, *Sisters in Crime: The Rise of the New Female Criminal*, New York: McGraw-Hill, 1975.

6 Otto Pollak, *The Criminality of Women*, Philadelphia: University of Pennsylvania Press, 1950.

7 B.K. Crew, "Sex Differences in Patriarchy: Chivalry or Patriarchy?" *Justice Quarterly*, vol. 8, no. 1, 1991.

8 See the collective work *Réflexions autour d'un tabou. L'infanticide*, Paris: Cambourakis, "Sorcières," 2015.

9 Coline Cardi, "Le féminin maternel ou la question du traitement pénal des femmes," *Pouvoirs*, no. 128, 2009; Mathilde Darley and Gwénaëlle Mainsant, "Police du genre," *Genèses*, no. 97, 2014.

10 See Cardi, "Le féminin maternel ou la question du traitement pénal des femmes."

11 For example: driving under the influence of alcohol, verbal assault, threat, theft, purchase of a stolen or counterfeit object, possession of an illegal drug, etc.

12 I am glossing over the debates raised by remand and judicial errors here, but they do supply powerful arguments to the abolitionist cause.

13 In both countries, the purchase of sexual services (by a client) is criminalized, but not the offer of sexual services. However, those who offer sex work are not protected from certain kinds of criminalization because of the informal nature of the profession, which obliges them to recoup certain expenses (such as rent) from third parties, who can be charged for pimping.

14 Joanne Belknap, *The Invisible Woman: Gender, Crime, and Justice*, Belmont: Wadsworth, 2001.

15 Arthur Vuattoux, "Les jeunes Roumaines sont des garçons comme les autres," *Plein droit,* no. 104, 2015.

16 Jamil Malakieh, *Statistiques sur les services correctionnels pour les adultes et les jeunes au Canada,* 2016–2017, Ottawa: Statistique Canada, 2018.

17 Karlene Faith, "La résistance à la pénalité: un impératif féministe," *Criminologie,* vol. 35, no. 2, 2002.

18 Meda Chesney-Lind and Noelie Rodriguez, "Women Under Lock and Key: A View From the Inside," *The Prison Journal,* vol. 63, no. 2, 1983; Meda Chesney-Lind and Randall G. Shelden, *Girls, Delinquency, and Juvenile Justice,* London: Wiley, 2014 [1992].

19 Malika Saada Saar, Rebecca Epstein, Lindsay Rosenthal and Yasmin Vafa, *The Sexual Abuse to Prison Pipeline: The Girls' Story,* Georgetown/Washington: Center for Poverty and Inequality/ Georgetown University Law Center, 2015.

20 Ibid.

21 Prison Reform Trust, *"There's a Reason We're in Trouble": Domestic Abuse as a Driver to Women's Offending,* London: Prison Reform Trust, 2017.

22 Angela Irvine, "We've Had Three of Them: Addressing the Invisibility of Lesbian, Gay, Bisexual, and Gender Nonconforming Youths in the Juvenile Justice System," *Columbia Journal of Gender and Law,* vol. 19, no. 3, 2010.

23 Ilan H. Meyer *et al.,* "Incarceration Rates and Traits of Sexual Minorities in the United States: National Inmate Survey, 2011– 2012," *American Journal of Public Health,* vol. 107, no. 2, 2017.

24 Estelle Freedman, "The Prison Lesbian: Race, Class and the Construction of the Aggressive Female Homosexual," *Feminist Studies,* vol. 22, no. 2, 1996.

25 Kathryn Ann Farr, "Defeminizing and Dehumanizing Female Murderers: Depictions of Lesbians on Death Row," *Women and Criminal Justice,* vol. 11, no. 1, 2000.

26 Charlotte Knight and Kath Wilson, *LGBT People and the Criminal Justice System,* London: Palgrave Macmillan, 2016.

27 The protests in support of Smith led to a pardon by President Bill Clinton in 2000.

28 Miriam Light, Eli Grant, and Kathryn Hopkins, *Gender Differences in Substance Misuse and Mental Health Amongst Prisoners. Results From the Surveying Prisoner Crime Reduction (SPCR) Longitudinal Cohort Study of Prisoners,* London: Ministry of Justice, 2013.

29 A task for which they are often called "mules."

30 Jennifer Fleetwood, *Drug Mules: Women in the International Cocaine Trade,* London: Palgrave Macmillan, 2014.

31 A revolutionary Marxist and feminist activist, Marilyn Buck

was arrested in 1985 for her involvement in armed struggle in the United States during the escape of the activist Assata Shakur in 1979. Sentenced to eighty years in prison, she died in 2010, less than one month after her compassionate release. During the twenty-five years she spent in prison, Marilyn Buck continued to organize and published numerous texts.

32   Marilyn Buck and Laura Whitehorn, "Cruel but Not Unusual: The Punishment of Women in US Prisons," in Joy James (ed.), *The New Abolitionists: Neo-slave Narratives and Contemporary Prison Writings*, Albany: SUNY Press, 2005, p. 232.

33   In other countries (for example, in US federal prisons), searches are sometimes performed by men.

34   The subject of how men and women are impacted differently by time served in prison is thoroughly examined in my own work. See Ricordeau, *Les détenus et leurs proches*.

35   In France, there are 42 correctional institutions for women and 179 for men.

36   Gwenola Ricordeau, "Sexualités féminines en prison: pratiques, discours et représentations," *Genre, sexualité et société*, no. 1, 2009; Myriam Joël-Lauf, "Coûts et bénéfices de l'homosexualité dans les prisons de femmes," *Ethnologie française*, vol. 43, no. 3, 2013.

37   Kathleen J. Ferraro and Angela M. Moe, "Mothering, Crime and Incarceration," *The Journal of Contemporary Ethnography*, vol. 32, no. 1, 2003.

38   Corinne Rostaing, *La relation carcérale. Identités et rapports sociaux dans les prisons de femmes*, Paris: Presses universitaires de France, "Le lien social" series, 1997.

39   Morgan Bassichis, *It's War in Here: A Report on the Treatment of Transgender and Intersex People in New York State Men's Prisons*, New York: Sylvia Rivera Law Project, 2007.

40   See, for the United States, Joey Mogul, Andrea Ritchie and Kay Whitlock, *Queer (In)justice: The Criminalization of LGBT People in the United States*, Boston: Beacon Press, 2011, p. 107–10.

41   Silpa Maruri, "Hormone Therapy for Inmates: A Metonym for Transgender Rights," *Cornell Journal of Law and Public Policy*, vol. 20, no. 3, 2010.

42   On trans people in Canadian prisons, see Allison Smith "Stories of Os: Transgender Women, Monstrous Bodies, and the Canadian Prison System," *Dalhousie Journal of Legal Studies*, vol. 23, 2014.

43   Lori Sexton, Valerie Jenness, and Jennifer Macy Sumner, "Where the Margins Meet: A Demographic Assessment of Transgender Inmates in Men's Prisons," *Justice Quarterly*, vol. 27, no. 6, 2010.

44   The majority of trans women in the Paris region have been placed in this jail since the mid-1990s following the reporting of a rape by

an inmate at the La Santé jail, which revealed the scope of sexual abuse suffered by trans and cross-dressing people in prison.

45 The primary law on prison matters adopted in France over a decade ago, which essentially lays out new provisions around sentencing and post-sentencing. See Corinne Rostaing, "L'invisibilisation des femmes dans les recherches sur la prison," *Les Cahiers de Framespa*, no. 25, 2017.

46 Coline Cardi, "La déviance des femmes: entre prison, justice et travail social," *Déviance et société*, vol. 31, no. 1, 2007.

47 Rose Giallombardo, *Society of Women: A Study of a Women's Prison*, New York: John Wiley & Sons, 1966.

48 Dvora Groman and Claude Faugeron, "Actualités bibliographiques. La criminalité féminine libérée: de quoi?" *Déviance et société*, vol. 3, no. 4, 1979.

49 Angela Davis, "Joan Little: The Dialectics of Rape," *Ms. Magazine*, vol. 3, no. 12, June 1975.

50 Meda Chesney-Lind, "Patriarchy, Crime, and Justice: Feminist Criminology in an Era of Backlash," *Feminist Criminology*, vol. 1, no. 1, 2006.

51 Rose Braz, "Kinder, Gentler, Gender Responsive Cages: Prison Expansion Is Not Prison Reform," in Russell Immarigeon (ed.), *Women and Girls in the Criminal Justice System: Policy Issues and Practice Strategies*, t. 2, Kingston, NJ: Civic Research Institute, 2006.

52 Term indicating the different treatment of men and women.

53 Patricia O'Brien and Debora M. Ortega, "Feminist Transformation. Deconstructing Prisons and Reconstructing Justice With Criminalized Women," *Affilia: Journal of Women and Social Work*, vol. 30, no. 2, 2015.

54 Jodie M. Lawston and Erica R. Meiners, "Ending Our Expertise: Feminists, Scholarship, and Prison Abolition," *Feminist Formations*, vol. 26, no. 2, 2014.

55 Kelly Hannah-Moffat, "Feminine Fortresses: Woman-Centered Prisons?" *The Prison Journal*, vol. 75, no. 2, 1995.

56 Brady T. Heinern and Sarah K. Tyson, "Feminism and the Carceral State: Gender-Responsive Justice, Community Accountability, and the Epistemology of Antiviolence," *Feminist Philosophy Quarterly*, vol. 3, no. 1, 2017.

57 Correctional Service Canada, *La création de choix: rapport du groupe d'étude sur les femmes purgeant une peine fédérale*, Ottawa: Ministry of Public Services and Procurement, 1990. For critical approaches, see Kelly Hannah-Moffat, *Punishment in Disguise: Penal Governance and Federal Imprisonment of Women in Canada*, Toronto: University of Toronto Press, 2001; Sylvie Frigon, "La création de choix pour les femmes incarcérées: sur les traces du

groupe d'étude sur les femmes purgeant une peine fédérale et de ses conséquences," *Criminologie,* vol. 35, no. 2, 2002.

58 Lawston and Meiners, "Ending Our Expertise."

59 Braz, "Kinder, Gentler, Gender Responsive Cages."

60 O'Brien and Ortega, "Feminist Transformation," pp. 142–3.

61 Julia Sudbury, "From Women Prisoners to People in Women's Prisons: Challenging the Gender Binary in Antiprison Work," in Jodie Michelle Lawston and Ashley E. Lucas (eds.), *Razor Wire Women: Prisoners, Activists, Scholars, and Artists,* Albany: SUNY Press, 2011.

62 Braz, "Kinder, Gentler, Gender Responsive Cages."

63 Cynthia Chandler, "The Gender-Responsive Prison Expansion Movement," in Rickie Solinger *et al.* (ed.), *Interrupted Life: Experiences of Incarcerated Women in the United States,* Berkeley: University of California Press, 2010.

64 Lawston, Meiners, "Ending Our Expertise."

65 Ibid., p. 10.

4. The Women at the Prison Gates

1 See Ricordeau, *Les détenus et leurs proches.*

2 I recommend the indispensable/vital book by Annie Livrozet (*Femme de voyou,* Paris, Lettres libres, 1983) and the documentary *À côté* (Stephane Mercurio, 2008) in which Chantal Courtois appears.

3 Duszka Maksymowicz's book *Femme de parloir* (Paris: L'Esprit frappeur, 2000) stands out in this genre.

4 Usually, the incarcerated loved one in question is a man.

5 Francine Cassan *et al.,* "L'histoire familiale des hommes détenus," *Synthèses,* no. 59, 2002.

6 Lloyd Withers and Jean Folsom, *Incarcerated Fathers: A Descriptive Analysis,* Ottawa: Correctional Service Canada, 2007.

7 Term designating women who fulfill a maternal role for a child who is not biologically related to them.

8 Patricia Hills Collins, *Black Feminist Thought: Knowledge, Consciousness, and the Politics of Empowerment,* New York/London: Routledge, 2009 [2000], p. 192 and following.

9 See Pierre Le Quéau (ed.), "*L'Autrepeine.*" *Enquête exploratoire sur les conditions de vie des familles de détenus,* Paris: CREDOC, 2000; INSEE, "L'histoire familiale des hommes détenus"; Caroline Touraut, *La famille à l'épreuve de la prison,* Paris: Presses universitaires de France, "Le lien social" series, 2012; as well as my own works, including *Les détenus et leurs proches.* The relatives

and friends of detained people have been the subject of much research in North America, see Meda Chesney-Lind and Marc Mauer (eds.), *Invisible Punishment: The Collateral Consequences of Mass Imprisonment,* New York: The New Press, 2002; Megan Comfort, *Doing Time Together: Love and Family in the Shadow of the Prison,* Chicago: University of Chicago Press, 2008.

10 Sandra Lehalle (ed.), "Les proches de personnes judiciarisées: expériences humaines et connaissances carcérales," *Criminologie,* vol. 52, no. 1, 2019.

11 In France, the profession has greatly evolved since from what had been known as "case workers," who helped incarcerated people in their efforts. Today, as reflected by their name (conseiller.e.s pénitentiaires d'insertion et de probation) they also have a role in evaluation and supervision in early release proceedings.

12 In France, the Collective de défense des familles et proches de personnes incarcérées (2001) is most notable, along with, more recently, the Association pour le respect des proches de personnes incarcérées (2008–9).

13 Le Quéau (ed.), "*L'Autre peine.*"

14 Ibid.

15 INSEE, "L'histoire familiale des hommes détenus."

16 On the mental health of relatives and friends of prisons in Canada, see Stacey Hannem and Louise Leonardi, *Forgotten Victims: The Mental Health and Well-Being of Families Affected by Crime and Incarceration in Canada,* Kingston: Canadian Families and Corrections Network, 2015.

17 Erving Goffman, *Stigmate. Les usages sociaux des handicaps,* Paris: Éditions de Minuit, "Le sens commun" series, 1975 [1963].

18 Denise Johnston and Megan Sullivan (eds.), *Parental Incarceration: Personal Accounts and Developmental Impact,* New York/London: Routledge, 2016.

19 Le Quéau (ed.), "*L'Autre peine.*"

20 Alvaro P. Pires, Pierre Landreville, and Victor Blankevoort, "Système pénal et trajectoire sociale," *Déviance et société,* vol. 5, no. 4, 1981.

21 Émile Durkheim, *De la division du travail social,* Paris: Presses universitaires de France, "Quadrige" series, 1996 [1893], pp. 35–78. *The Division of Labour in Society* (1893)

22 Incite!, *The Revolution Will Not Be Funded: Beyond the Non-Profit Industrial Complex,* Durham, NC: Duke University Press, 2017 [2007]. Incite! is a group in the United States founded in 2000 and composed of women of color and trans people. Its full name is Incite! Women and Trans People of Color Against Violence. "Trans People" does not appear in its earliest publications. See chapter 6 for more on the group's contributions to the development of transformative justice.

23 Jacques Donzelot, *La police des familles*, Paris: Éditions de Minuit, "Reprise" series, 2005 [1977].

24 No one asks these women what the meaning of this word is, when they witness each day how prison works to "disintegrate" their relatives and friends.

25 On the forms of stigmatization of relatives and friends of prisoners in Canada, see Stacey Hannem, "Stigma and Marginality: Gendered Experiences of Families of Male Prisoners in Canada," in Aaron Doyle and Dawn Moore (eds.), *Critical Criminology in Canada: New Voices, New Directions*, Vancouever/Toronto: UBC Press, 2011.

26 For Canada, see Kaitlin MacKenzie, "'La seule constance... c'est l'inconstance.' Les répercussions des faux positifs des scanneurs à ions sur les familles des détenus canadiens," *Criminologie*, vol. 52, no. 1, 2019.

27 See Gwenola Ricordeau and Régis Schlagdenhauffen (eds.), "Sexualités et institutions pénales," *Champ pénal/Penal Field*, vol. 13, 2016.

28 In Canada, prisoners have access every two months to private family visits of seventy-two hours (see Marion Vacheret, "Les visites familiales privées au Canada, entre réinsertion et contrôle accru: portrait d'un système," *Champ pénal/Penal Field*, vol. 2, 2005). In France, out of nearly 200 correctional institutions, only twenty-six have family visit units (apartments intended for private visits of forty-eight to seventy-two hours) and nine have intimate visiting rooms (private rooms for visits of a maximum six hours).

29 See "Additional Resources" (pp. 155–6), and, especially, Soledad *et al.*, *Guide à l'usage des proches de personnes incarcérées*, Paris, 2013, written by relatives and friends of prisoners.

30 See the work of the US sociologist Megan Comfort: "'C'est plein de mecs bien en taule!' Incarcération de masse aux États-Unis et ambivalence des épouses," *Actes de la recherche en sciences sociales*, vol. 4, no. 169, 2007.

5. Penal Abolitionism and Feminism

1 See note 58 on p. 161. This period is marked by fights for women's suffrage, but also to education, work, and birth control.

2 See Estelle Freedman, *Their Sisters' Keepers: Women's Prison Reform in America, 1830–1930*, Ann Arbor: University of Michigan Press, 1981; Nicole Hahn Rafter, *Partial Justice: Women in State Prisons, 1800–1935*, Boston: Northeastern University Press, 1985.

3 Simone de Beauvoir, *The Second Sex*, transl. Constance Borde and Sheila Malovany-Chevallier, New York: Vintage, 2009, p. 8.

4 Karlene Faith, "La résistance à la pénalité: un impératif féministe," *Criminologie*, vol. 35, no. 2, 2002.

5 The term "carceralism" encapsulates the ideology that, beyond simple legitimism, advocates for prison sentences as the solution to social problems.

6 Elizabeth Bernstein, "Carceral Politics as Gender Justice? The 'Traffic in Women' and Neoliberal Circuits of Crime, Sex, and Rights," *Theory and Society,* vol. 41, no. 3, 2012, p. 235.

7 Roger N. Lancaster, *Sex Panic and the Punitive State*, Berkeley: University of California Press, 2011.

8 Elizabeth Bernstein, "The Sexual Politics of New Abolitionism," *Differences*, vol. 18, no. 3, 2007; "Militarized Humanitarianism Meets Carceral Feminism: The Politics of Sex, Rights, and Freedom in Contemporary Anti-Trafficking Campaigns," *Signs*, vol. 36, no. 1, 2010.

9 Bernstein, "Carceral Politics as Gender Justice?"

10 See Jean Bérard, *La justice en procès. Les mouvements de contestation face au système pénal (1968–1983)*, Paris: Presses de Sciences Po, 2013, pp. 229–51.

11 Kristin Bumiller, *In an Abusive State: How Neoliberalism Appropriated the Feminist Movement Against Sexual Violence*, Durham, NC: Duke University Press, 2008.

12 Voir Bernstein, "Carceral Politics as Gender Justice?"

13 Bérard, *La justice en procès*, pp. 160–79.

14 Agnès Ouin, "La violence de la justice," *Déviance et société*, vol. 3, no. 1, 1979.

15 Beth E. Richie, "A Black Feminist Reflection on the Antiviolence Movement," *Signs*, vol. 25, no. 4, 2000; Erica R. Meiners, "Never Innocent: Feminist Trouble With Sex Offender Registries and Protection in a Prison Nation," *Meridians*, vol. 9, no. 2, 2009, p. 34.

16 Beth E. Richie, *Arrested Justice: Black Women, Violence, and America's Prison Nation*, New York: NYU Press, 2012.

17 Incite!, "Gender Violence and the Prison Industrial Complex," in CR10 Publication Collective, *Abolition Now! Ten Years of Strategy and Struggle Against the Prison Industrial Complex*, Oakland: AK Press, 2008 [2001], p. 21.

18 John Pratt, Penal Populism, New York, Routledge, 2005; Denis Salas, *La volonté de punir. Essai sur le populisme pénal*, Paris: Hachette, "Pluriel" series, 2005.

19 "Carceral feminisms," should also be mentioned, as suggested by Elizabeth Whalley and Colleen Hackett ("Carceral Feminisms: The Abolitionist Project and Undoing Dominant Feminisms," *Contemporary Justice Review*, vol. 20, no. 4, 2017).

20 Chloë Taylor, "Anti-Carceral Feminism and Sexual Assault—a Defense: A Critique of the Critique of the Critique of Carceral Feminism," *Social Philosophy Today,* vol. 34, 2018.

21 Lise Gotell, "Reassessing the Place of Criminal Law Reform in the Struggle Against Sexual Violence: A Critique of the Critique of Carceral Feminism," in Anastasia Powell, Nicola Henry, and Asher Flynn (eds.), *Rape Justice: Beyond the Criminal Law,* New York: Palgrave Macmillan, 2015.

22 Morgan Bassichis, Alexander Lee, and Dean Spade, "Building an Abolitionist Trans and Queer Movement With Everything We've Got," in Eric A. Stanley and Nat Smith (eds.), *Captive Genders: Trans Embodiment and the Prison Industrial Complex,* Oakland: AK Press, 2011.

23 For recent developments, see Viviane Saleh-Hanna, "Black Feminist Hauntology," *Champ pénal/Penal Field,* vol. 12, 2015.

24 See Emily Thuma, "Lessons in Self-Defense: Gender Violence, Racial Criminalization, and Anticarceral Feminism," *Women's Studies Quarterly,* vol. 43, nos. 3–4, 2015.

25 Harold E. Pepinsky, "The Contribution of Feminist Justice to Criminology," *Feminist Teacher,* vol. 4, no. 1, 1989; René van Swaaningen "Feminism and Abolitionism as Critiques of Criminology," *International Journal of the Sociology of Law,* vol. 17, no. 3, 1989.

26 Brian D. MacLean and Harold E. Pepinsky (eds.), *We Who Would Take No Prisoners: Selections From the Fifth International Conference on Penal Abolition,* Vancouver: Collective Press, 1993, p. 10.

27 Beth Richie, "Queering Anti-Prison Work: African American Lesbians in the Juvenile Justice System," in Julia Sudbury (ed.), *Global Lockdown: Race, Gender, and the Prison-Industrial Complex,* New York: Routledge, 2005; Eric Stanley, Dean Spade, and Queer (In)Justice, "Queering Prison Abolition, Now?" *American Quarterly,* vol. 64, no. 1, 2012.

28 Stanley and Smith (eds.), *Captive Genders.*

29 Bassichis, Lee, and Spade, "Building an Abolitionist, Trans and Queer Movement With Everything We've Got."

30 Term designating the communication strategies (of companies, of States, etc.) that utilize the promotion of LGBTQ rights and aid to LGBTQ communities to construct a progressive image.

31 Melanie Brazzell, "Was macht uns sicher? Die Polizei jedenfalls nicht der Transformative-Justice-Ansatz," *Analyse & Kritik,* no. 621, 2016.

32 On these collectives, see Bassichis, Lee, and Spade, "Building an Abolitionist Trans and Queer Movement With Everything We've Got"; Lisa Guenther and Chloë Taylor, "Introduction: Queer, Trans,

and Feminist Responses to the Prison Nation," *philoSOPHIA*, vol. 6, no. 1, 2016.

33 Ryan Conrad, *Against Equality: Prisons Will Not Protect You*, Lewiston, ME: Against Equality Press, 2012.

34 Bassichis, Lee, and Spade, "Building an Abolitionist Trans and Queer Movement With Everything We've Got."

35 Vanessa R. Panfil, *The Gang's All Queer*.

36 The video is available for viewing at vimeo.com/234353103. A full transcript of the speech is here: issuu.com/shadesofnoir/docs/peekaboo_we_see_you_whiteness/s/151964.

37 Martin D. Schwartz and Walter S. DeKeseredy, "Left Realist Criminology: Strengths, Weaknesses and the Feminist Critique," *Crime, Law and Social Change*, vol. 15, no. 1, 1991, p. 62.

38 Incite! "Gender Violence and the Prison Industrial Complex."

39 Adina Ilea, "What About 'the Sex Offenders'? Addressing Sexual Harm From an Abolitionist Perspective," *Critical Criminology*, vol. 26, no. 3, 2018.

40 Victoria Law, *Resistance Behind Bars: The Struggles of Incarcerated Women*, Oakland: PM Press, 2009, p. 5.

41 The expression was coined by Grégory Salle, see "Situations(s) carcérale(s) en Allemagne. Prison et politique," *Déviance et société*, vol. 27, no. 4, 2003, p. 406.

42 A term designating the revolutionary theories and strategies favoring recourse to insurrection (rebellions, riots, etc.) rather than other forms of organization (for example, in a party or union).

43 Michel Foucault very accurately addresses this question in his introduction to Serge Livrozet's book (*De la prison à la révolte*, Paris, L'Esprit frappeur, 1999 [1973], pp. 5–13).

44 From the word "token," the term designates the practice of including and rendering visible a person of a minority group (woman, person of color, etc.) in a symbolic manner.

45 Gwenola Ricordeau, "No. Abolitionist Movement Without Us! Manifesto for Prisoners' Relatives and Friends," in Massimo Pavarini et Livio Ferrari (ed.), *No Prison*, London: EG Press, 2018.

46 Joy is not absent from the prison gates and I regret that activist culture is so cruelly lacking in it when it comes to fighting against prison. No doubt because of the biases of people who have never experienced it and who struggle to imagine prison as an intensely vibrant place, one where joy might be possible.

47 The misogynistic association of women with submissive and passive behaviors does not merit more attention here.

48 Jodie Michelle Lawston, "'We're All Sisters': Bridging and Legitimacy in the Women's Antiprison Movement," *Gender and Society*,

vol. 23, no. 5, 2009; and *Sisters Outside: Radical Activists Working for Women Prisoners,* Albany: SUNY Press, 2010.

49 For example, a certain form of negligence with regard to clothing (in many radical white and intellectual milieus) *versus* the dignity associated with physical appearance and with clothing brands (in particular in prison).

50 Notably the way in which the formal and informal rules (agenda, turns to speak, etc.) are socially and culturally situated.

6. Emancipating Ourselves From the Criminal Justice System and Constructing Autonomy

1 The term, intended here in its sociological sense, designates, without being judgmental, the transgression of a social norm.

2 Émile Durkheim, *Les règles de la méthode sociologique,* Paris: Presses universitaires de France, "Quadrige" series, 1993 [1895]. *The Rules of Sociological Method*

3 On the offenses for which women are incarcerated, see chapter 2.

4 Meda Chesney-Lind, "Patriarchy, Prisons, and Jails: A Critical Look at Trends in Women's Incarceration," *The Prison Journal,* vol. 71, no. 1, 1991.

5 Morgan Bassichis, Alexander Lee, and Dean Spade, "Building an Abolitionist Trans and Queer Movement With Everything We've Got," in Eric A. Stanley and Nat Smith (eds.), *Captive Genders: Trans Embodiment and the Prison Industrial Complex,* Oakland: AK Press, 2011.

6 Pat Carlen, *Alternatives to Women's Imprisonment,* Milton Keynes: Open University Press, 1990, p. 121.

7 Fay Honey Knopp, *Retraining Adult Sex Abusers: Methods and Models,* Syracuse: Safer Society Press, 1984.

8 Fay Honey Knopp, "On Radical Feminism and Abolition," *Peace Review,* vol. 6, no. 2, 1994, p. 59.

9 See cosacanada.com.

10 Adina Ilea, "What About 'the Sex Offenders'? Addressing Sexual Harm From an Abolitionist Perspective," *Critical Criminology,* vol. 26, no. 3, 2018.

11 Ian A. Elliott and Gary Zajac, "The Implementation of Circles of Support and Accountability in the United States," *Aggression and Violent Behavior,* vol. 25, 2015.

12 Robin J. Wilson, Franca Cortoni, and Andrew J. McWhinnie, "Circles of Support & Accountability: A Canadian National Replication of Outcome Findings," *Sexual Abuse,* vol. 21, no. 4, 2009.

13 Those who make these critiques would surely do better to worry about the accessibility of women, people of color, or people with disabilities to these same social spaces.

14 Victoria Law, "Where Abolition Meets Action: Women Organizing Against Gender Violence," *Contemporary Justice Review*, vol. 14, no. 1, 2011.

15 For a synthesis of the feminist critique of international criminal justice, see Julien Pieret "Une justice pénale internationale vue par les femmes: continuités et bifurcations dans les analyses féministes de la pénalité," *Champ pénal/Penal Field*, vol. 13, 2016.

16 The most well known is the Permanent Peoples' Tribunal (PPT). It was inspired by the international tribunal against war crimes committed in Vietnam, which was held in 1966–7 on the initiative of the British philosopher Bertrand Russell and the French intellectual and activist Jean-Paul Sartre.

17 Such as that established by the Truth and Reconciliation Commission in South Africa after apartheid.

18 See Jennifer Matsunaga, "Two Faces of Transitional Justice: Theorizing the Incommensurability of Transitional Justice and Decolonization in Canada," *Decolonization: Indigeneity, Education & Society*, vol. 5, no. 1, 2016; Rosemary L. Nagy, "The Scope and Bounds of Transitional Justice and the Canadian Truth and Reconciliation Commission," *International Journal of Transitional Justice*, vol. 7, no. 1, 2012.

19 See M. Kay Harris, "Transformative Justice: The Transformation of Restorative Justice," in Dennis Sullivan and Larry Tifft (eds.), *Handbook of Restorative Justice: A Global Perspective*, London: Routledge, 2006.

20 John Braithwaite, *Crime, Shame and Reintegration*, Cambridge: Cambridge University Press, 1989.

21 Barbara Hudson, "Restorative Justice and Gendered Violence: Diversion or Effective Justice?" *British Journal of Criminology*, vol. 42, no. 3, 2002; Julie Stubbs, "Domestic Violence and Women's Safety: Feminist Challenges to Restorative Justice," in Heather Strang and John Braithwaite (eds.), *Restorative Justice and Family Violence*, Cambridge: Cambridge University Press, 2002.

22 C. Quince Hopkins et Mary P. Koss, "Incorporating Feminist Theory and Insights Into a Restorative Justice Response to Sex Offenses," *Violence Against Women*, vol. 11, no. 5, 2005.

23 Harold E. Pepinsky and Richard Quinney, *Criminology as Peacemaking*, Bloomington: Indiana University Press, 1991.

24 Howard Zehr, *Changing Lenses: A New Focus for Crime and Justice*, Scottdale: Herald Press, 1990.

25 An Evangelical and Anabaptist Christian movement.

26 See Véronique Strimelle, "La justice restaurative: une innovation du pénal?" *Champ pénal/Penal Field*, vol. 5, 2007.

27 Beyond the analyses that these different groups have produced, see Ana Clarissa Rojas Durazo, Alissa Bierria, and Mimi Kim (eds.), "Community Accountability: Emerging Movements to Transform Violence," *Social Justice*, vol. 37, no. 4, 2012.

28 Ruth Morris, *Stories of Transformative Justice*, Toronto: Canadian Scholars' Press, 2000.

29 See the Centre de services de justice réparatrice: csjr.org/fr.

30 Sophia Boutilier and Lana Wells, *The Case for Reparative and Transformative Justice Approaches to Sexual Violence in Canada: A Proposal to Pilot and Test New Approaches*, Calgary: University of Calgary/Shift: The Project to End Domestic Violence, 2018.

31 See Mimi E. Kim, "Moving Beyond Critique: Creative Interventions and Reconstructions of Community Accountability," *Social Justice*, vol. 37, no. 4, 2012.

32 The term two-spirit, specific to Indigenous North American cultures, designates people who identify as having both a masculine and a feminine spirit.

33 Creative Interventions, *Creative Interventions Toolkit: A Practical Guide to Stop Interpersonal Violence*, 2012, creative-interventions.org/wp-content/uploads/2012/06/CI-Toolkit-Complete-Pre-Release-Version-06.2012-.pdf.

34 generationFIVE, *Toward Transformative Justice: A Liberatory Approach to Child Sexual Abuse and Other Forms of Intimate and Community Violence*, 2007, generationfive.org/wp-content/uploads/2013/07/G5_Toward_Transformative_Justice-Document.pdf.

35 Louk Hulsman, "Struggles about Terminology: 'Problematic Situation' vs. 'Crime'," in Yves Cartuyvels *et al.* (eds.), *Politique, police et justice au bord du futur. Mélanges pour et avec Lode Van Outrive*, Paris: L'Harmattan, 1998.

36 Chrysalis Collective, "Beautiful, Difficult, Powerful: Ending Sexual Assault Through Transformative Justice," in Ching-In Chen, Jai Dulani, and Leah Lakshmi Piepzna-Samarasinha (eds.), *The Revolution Starts at Home: Confronting Intimate Violence Within Activist Communities*, Cambridge: South End Press, 2011.

37 Chen, Dulani and Lakshmi Piepzna-Samarasinha (eds.), *The Revolution Starts at Home*.

38 See chapter 2 and specifically Ilea, "What About 'the Sex Offenders?'"

39 CARA, "Taking Risks: Implementing Grassroots Community Accountability Strategies," in Incite!, *The Revolution Will Not Be Funded: Beyond the Non-Profit Industrial Complex*, Cambridge: South End Press, 2006, p. 251.

40 See Gaurav Jashnani, R.J. Maccani, and Alan Greig, "What Does It Feel Like When Change Finally Comes? Male Supremacy, Accountability & Transformative Justice," in Chen, Dulani and Lakshmi Piepzna-Samarasinha (eds.), *The Revolution Starts at Home.*

41 For constructive critiques of TJ practices, see A.J. Withers, *Transformative Justice and/as Harm,* Toronto: Rebuild Printing, 2014, stillmyrevolution.files.wordpress.com/2015/12/tj-zine-final-with-cover.pdf.

42 See Karlene Faith, "Aboriginal Women's Healing Lodge: Challenge to Penal Correctionalism?" *Journal of Human Justice,* vol. 6, no. 2, 1995.

43 Mylène Jaccoud, "Les cercles de guérison et les cercles de sentence autochtones au Canada," *Criminologie,* vol. 32, no. 1, 1999.

44 Kimberlé W. Crenshaw, "From Private Violence to Mass Incarceration: Thinking Intersectionally About Women, Race, and Social Control," *UCLA Law Review,* vol. 59, no. 6, 2012.

45 Soledad *et al.*, *Guide à l'usage des proches de personnes incarcérées,* Paris, 2013.

46 I owe the discovery of this concept to a meeting with Adel Samara, a Palestinian activist, and to the reading of his *Epidemic of Globalization: Ventures in World Oder, Arab Nation and Zionism* (Glendale: Palestine Research and Publishing Foundation, 2005). The use of this term is now widespread: we find it, in 2014, used by the Indian writer and activist Arundhati Roy (*The End of Imagination,* Chicago: Haymarket Books, 2016).

47 The expression "double shift" refers to the fact that, in heterosexual couples, women carry out most domestic tasks while also, for the majority, being salaried employees.

48 Julia Sudbury, "Building a Movement to Abolish Prisons: Lessons from the U.S.," *Journal of Prisoners on Prisons,* vol. 18, nos. 1–2, 2009, p. 182.

49 See Joël Charbit and Gwenola Ricordeau, "Au risque de la participation: comparaison des syndicats de prisonniers en France et aux États-Unis," *Participations,* vol. 3, no. 22, 2018.

50 The slogan "If the 'innocent' deserve our solidarity, the 'guilty' deserve it even more" from the Anarchist Black Cross (an international organization in support of prisoners and political prisoners) perfectly illustrates the critique of innocentism by abolitionist movements.

Epilogue

1 Thomas Mathiesen, *The Politics of Abolition Revisited*, London: Routledge, 2015 [1974].